The Malinois

Jan Kaldenbach

D1512043

Detselig Enterprises Ltd.

Calgary, Alberta, Canada

The Malinois

© 1997 Jan Kaldenbach

Canadian Cataloguing in Publication Data

Kaldenbach, Jan
  The malinois

Includes index.
ISBN 1-55059-151-7

  1. Belgian malinois. 2. Police dogs—Holland. I. Title
SF 429.B4K34   1997   636.7'37   C97-910025-9

Detselig Enterprises Ltd.
210-1220 Kensington Rd. N.W.
Calgary, Alberta T2N 3P5

  Detselig Enterprises Ltd. appreciates the financial support
for our 1997 publishing program, provided by Canadian Heri-
tage and the Alberta Foundation for the Arts, a beneficiary of
the Lottery Fund of the Government of Alberta.

Printed in Canada
ISBN 1-55059-151-7
SAN 115-0324

Cover design by Dean Macdonald.

Table of Contents

f) Position Exercises

g) General Obedience and the Way to
   Present the Dog

h) KNPV Certificates

a) The Dog as a Means of Warning

b) The Dog as a Weapon

c) The Dog as a Means of Tracking

Introduction

I am writing this book after much prompting from friends throughout Germany, Canada and the United States. For years they have complained about the lack of information available (especially in English) on the Malinois as a breed, and more importantly, on the Malinois as a working dog.

This book then, is an in-depth look at the Malinois, its background, breed characteristics, training and usefulness as a police service dog. And of course, to discuss the Malinois without explaining the involvement of the KNPV (the Royal Dutch Police Dog Society) would not do justice to the development of the breed.

The society began as a standard-setting agency for all police service dogs in Holland. National interest from civilians, however, became so strong that in 1932 the KNPV split and became two separate entities. The civilian sector continued with the KNPV and the police founded the Netherlands Association for the Service Dog. Both did police dog work until 1995, but since then, only the government can examine dogs for the police service.

The properly bred Malinois is an excellent dog with whom you can do many things. But a good dog is more than just breeding, it must be properly trained as well. My favorite answer to all my American and Canadian friends is "The good ones do not grow on trees. You cannot simply pick them as you may a piece of fruit!"

Jan Kaldenbach

About the Author . . .

Jan Kaldenbach is a retired Lieutenant of the Zaanstad Police Department in The Netherlands. He has published numerous articles in Dutch on the subject of K9 training and use, and articles in English in *Dogs Against Drugs/Dogs Against Crime* and in *The Quarterly*, the magazine of the Canadian Police Canine Association.

He is a top breeder of Belgian Malinois and other breeds and has provided police dogs to a number of police departments in Canada and the U.S. The absolute top dog among them was Prince, a German Shepherd working in Lansing, Illinois, who found $5 million U.S. worth of drug money in a car. Other top dogs are also mentioned throughout this book.

He has taken part, as an instructor, in a variety of seminars and demonstrations for K9 handlers and trainers, including several DAD/DAC seminars in the United States, and a seminar with Bob Eden on Vancouver Island in Canada. He has also been invited to provide briefings to dog handlers of the U.S. Secret Service in Washington, D.C., while visiting the White House, and to detector dog handlers in Bryansk, Russia. He was an advisor to the Vero Beach, Florida, police department for three days, and was invited in January 1997 by the Head of the CID of the Dubai Police Department in the United Arab Emirates to advise on the upgrading of their dog unit.

Mr. Kaldenbach has been invited numerous times by the German Police to assist in suspect discrimination using police dogs. On a number of occasions, he has been the guest of honor at the International Games for Police Dog Handlers held in various locations in Germany.

Jan Kaldenbach currently resides in The Netherlands.

1

The Malinois and its Origins

Beginnings

During the latter part of the last century, countries throughout Western Europe went through tremendous industrial development. Because of this development, there was an increase in the number of wealthy, with a corresponding increase in leisure time, and the interest in raising dogs of various breeds and types became greater.

There were already many kinds of sheep dog from various backgrounds. The sizes of these breeds were fairly similar, approximately fifty centimetres high, with a build that was typically square and fine-boned. They were excellent help for the shepherd, but were tempermental and wary of strangers. They were work dogs of tremendous form and overall structure and could work in all kinds of weather. They worked the herds as if it was their joy in life.

At the end of the last century it became fashionable to raise dogs. This was when Cynologique had its beginning and people began to exhibit dogs. The working dogs of the land, however, were not included. The exhibiting of working dogs, all herding dogs, came later. Cynologique was in the hands of the wealthy classes. They tended to acquire their dogs from outside the country and they tried to outdo one another with breeds from several countries. Also, there were not very many shepherds

---

Editor's Note: for convenience and smoother reading, we have elected to use the pronouns "he, him, his" when referring to the dog, the handler or the decoy, rather than the more academic, and awkward, "he/she, him/her, his/hers."

who were willing to bring their dogs into competitions to have them tested and to exhibit them.

A very well-known professor, Dr. Reul, had worked with the Belgian Shepherd and in 1891 he succeeded in bringing more than one hundred Belgian Shepherds together. Information was slowly gathered and many years later, just before the close of the nineteenth century, a list was completed of breed characteristics, which such dogs had to match in order to qualify for showing and pedigree. There was now a broader view of this breed and a distinction among three hair breeds. The first was the short-haired Mechelse or Malinois Shepherd; the second group was the long-haired black Groenendaeler and the red-brown Tervuerense Shepherd; and the third was the rough-haired or the Laekense Shepherd. From that time on the Mechelse Shepherd, or Malinois, was recognized as a breed.

Professor Reul continued his research on this Belgian Shepherd breed, but it took a very long time before the first two varieties could be written into the Belgian dog register. The royal society, St. Hubertus, would not allow the entrance of the Belgian Shepherd breed into the dog register. This honor was reserved only for dignified breeds, such as the Collie and the Barzoi, which of course belonged to the very well-to-do ladies and gentlemen.

However, slowly but surely, the Belgian Shepherd breeds, which were later called Work Dog breeds, also received more recognition. The short-haired Belgian Sheepdog, also known as the Short-haired Shepherd, developed into its best form in the region of Brabantse Kempen, in the neighborhood of the Dutch border, and then also developed further in the Dutch province of Noord-Brabant. Professor Reul was influential in setting standards for the build and height development by way of breeding. He was also influential in the beginning of a club in Mechelen in Belgium, just south of the the Netherlands, in 1898, known as the Mechelse Club for Improvement of the Short-Haired Sheepdog. It was accepted as a division of the *Club de Chien de Berger Belge* (The Belgian Shepherd Dog Club). The goal of this club was to improve the breed, which was soon to be called the Mechelaar or Malinois. The different names result from both Dutch and French being spoken in Belgium — thus Mechelaar for the Dutch, and Malinois for the French.

The rise of the popularity of the Malinois among breeders did not come easily. Opinions on the goals of Belgian Shepherd breeding varied and there were many misunderstandings, resulting in a slower recognition of this breed. The opinions expressed in the Mechelse Club varied from those of the *Club de Chien de Berger Belge* in that the Mechelse Club considered the inner temperament of the dog very important, in addition to the outward appearance. They demanded that the Mechelaar be work dogs. As I write this, it occurs to me that nothing much has changed in the dog breeding world. These differences of opinion over beauty and character still exist, but the greater attention to character has resulted in more well-balanced dogs.

Development

Considerable effort, in the form of organized competitions held nowhere else in the world, helped to bring out the breed's best qualities and to provide world-wide recognition of the quality Malinois. Also, there was a concerted effort to hold contests for guard and attack-defense dogs. General guidelines and rules had to be established. Many demonstrations were held, emphasizing the Mechelaars. The first public contest was held in Mechelen (of course) in 1903. The first prize was awarded to a Mechelse Shepherd female named Cora, owned by a Mr. Opdebeeck. He was a Malinois breeder from Mechelen. Thus Cora is the ancestress of the present Malinois.

Cora was mated with Tomy from Brussels. She and he are the recognized parents of the Malinois breed. Tomy was a beautiful male dog, red-brown with a black mask, such as you see in today's dog. One of the descendants of Cora and Tomy was Tjop, a rough-haired Malinois, who belonged to a shepherd who was allowed to graze his sheep in the gardens of the royal palace in Leaken, by Brussels, the Belgian capital. He was an excellent representative of the breed, however, there was some criticism during a competition, because of the build of the dog, and this caused considerable commotion. Another Malinois, Dewet, was prettier and more perfect. There were many hearty discussions, but the result was that Tjop was first awarded the "Laekense Herder" championship and Dewet disappeared from view.

Both types, however, have been very important for the development of the Malinois. There was constant breeding, either with one or the other or with both dogs. After the first World War, the breed had to be corrected a little bit again. Belgium was involved in the war, whereas the Netherlands was neutral. The dogs came heavily into use in battle situations, and in order to reinstitute a breeding population, the Malinois were for a short time bred with other dogs. After the war, dogs appeared that had more color variations. Successful corrections resulted in the original colors being reinstated in the breed.

The time between the first and second World Wars was used to further the development of the breed. During the second World War, however, many dogs, as well as humans, suffered and many of the best of the Malinois breed were lost due to a lack of good food for both humans and animals. I remember very well how the dogs had to eat whatever was available, often what was left over from the families' meals. Today the dog food is good and the dogs are well cared for.

Character

The time after World War II was used to bring the dog back to its original luster. That beauty was brought back and is still here today. Often the desire to raise beautiful dogs created serious disturbances in the building up of character in the dogs. It is always very important to raise Malinois for their character. My belief is that beauty must come in second place. After all, the Malinois is a work dog.

"Barry" was a mixed Malinois. His character was found to be unsuitable for police work.

Members in the dog sporting world, for instance the KNPV, prefer to use a Malinois cross. These dogs are not always as beautiful, but certainly effective. One is expected to trade a little beauty for a certain character!

This book, then, is about the usefulness and the application of the Malinois in training and practice. In the Netherlands, the Malinois is the breed that rings bells in the dog sporting world. Other breeds can really be neglected. Here, the Malinois can be employed anywhere – as a tracking dog or as a surveillance dog. The Malinois has just as good a nose as that of other breeds, including the German Shepherd, and is at least as, if not more, motivated. I must add that I hold the German Shepherd in high respect. It has gone through excellent development and is, as a police dog, very worthwhile. My German Shepherd detector dogs, Tim and Astor, were excellent dogs and, through the use of their well-developed noses, were quite successful in fighting crime.

The Malinois are now in their prime and many of these, pedigreed and not, are now found in the police service. The work that has been done in the past to bring out the drives and instincts necessary for an effective Police Service Dog have now brought the dog to a satisfactory point.

As expected, there are still disagreements today between the various breed organizations. Dog people, because they have to remain in control of the dog, are by nature domineering. As a result, dog breeders and dog handlers do not always relate well to one another or to the general public, mainly because the public buys the dog as a pet, not realizing that the differences in the breeding of work dogs and show dogs, as opposed to pets, can make the former less than satisfying as a household friend. But in spite the bickering and controversy, a breed developed which became a very good, useful dog. This breed is the Malinois.

It is an art to consolidate from past work with this breed and to build on it for the future.

My first patrol dog, "Astor I", in 1964. With this dog, a mixed Malinois, I got my first KNPV certificate. The dog died in 1967, of cancer. The dog worked so well that he was the basis for my later success as a dog handler. Many other Malinois became members of my dog unit later on.

2

Present Characteristics of the Breed

Before discussing the characteristics of the Malinois breed, I must emphasize the fact that the Malinois, in the police dog world, consists of two kinds of dogs. These are the ones with a pedigree and the ones without a pedigree, the latter outnumbering the former.

The pedigreed Malinois is a graceful, beautiful dog, and what it loses in size it more than makes up in character and heart. The one without a pedigree has a thousand faces. Cross breeding Malinois with German Shepherds, Dutch Shepherds, Boxers and Great Danes has given the Malinois the best characteristics of all the breeds to withstand the stresses and challenges of being a police service dog.

If you decide to get a Malinois, do not rigidly compare it with the breed characteristics, as you will be disappointed. That is, "you will come home from a cold carnival" as the Dutch would say. I am talking here about the beauty, the looks of the dog.

However, with the character it is something completely different, and sometimes just the opposite. The non-pedigreed dog often has the characteristics necessary for training. A cross-bred Malinois is very useful and, here in Holland, very much appreciated by friend and very much feared by foe. Often, because of the cross-breeding of the non-pedigreed Malinois, larger specimens result than by breeding pedigreed Malinois Shepherds.

The larger dogs are more in demand by the police because they are more intimidating and act as greater deterrents. However, the breed characteristics are as follows.

Common Appearances and Qualities

The dog is a medium-sized, harmoniously-shaped, intelligent and sturdy animal, used to living in the open air and built to withstand the various temperatures and weather and the many changes of seasons. Because of this harmony in appearance and the proud, high-held head, the Malinois gives the impression of elegant strength, which became the inheritance of the royal representatives of the work dog breeds. Next to his inborn ability as a herd dog, he has all the qualifications of the very best watchdog, and without hesitation, he is one of the toughest and fiercest defenders of his boss. He is watchful and attentive. His spirit and questioning look serve as testimony to his intelligence.

"Athos de la Tourbiere" – now working as a police dog in Honolulu.

The Head

The head is delicately cut, long without exaggeration and not fleshy. The skull and snout are about the same length with no more than a small difference which enhances the length of the snout. The dog's refined facial features also emphasize the delicate details of the complete dog.

Skull

Medium width in comparison to the length of the head. The forehead is more flat than rounded, with not much distinction of the forehead slope. Looking at it from the side, it runs parallel with the imaginary line which makes the snout longer.

Ears

They are clearly three-sided, stiff and carried straight up. Their inset is high, and they are proportioned in size. The oracles (shell of the ear) are rounded nicely from the base.

Eyes

They are of medium size, without bulging or laying too deep. They are light almond in form, brownish, preferably darker of color, and the eyelids have a black edge. The look is bright, lively, intelligent and questioning.

The Eyebrows

Not sticking out. The snout is well cut under the eyes.

Nose Mirror

The face, or flat part of the nose, should be black with good-sized, open nostrils.

Snout

Medium of length, the snout gets narrower as it gets closer to the nose. The bridge of the nose is straight. Looking at it from the sides, it is parallel with the imaginary line drawn from the skull. The mouth is good-sized, to allow the dog to carry objects comfortably.

Cheeks

Not fleshy or loose-skinned, very flat, with pronounced musculature.

Lips

They are thin-skinned, they close well, have a definite color and don't show the red of the mucous membranes.

Teeth

The jaws are strong with very white teeth, implanted evenly and strongly in good developed jaw bones. The dog can scissor-bite with the teeth of the upper jaw sliding into the ones from the bottom jaw without leaving any gaps, which is called *Schaargebit*. Cutting teeth overbite, and the so-called eye teeth are allowed.

The Stop

The indentation between the forehead and the nose should have a moderate angle.

Throat

Stands out very nicely. The throat is a little long, well-muscled without any skin hanging, gradually getting broader towards the shoulders.

Neck

Bent very slightly.

Shoulders

Seen from the side, the shoulder blades are long and slanted. They lay flat and form, along with the upper arm bone, a good angle by which the free working of the elbows is assured.

Upper arms

Must be able to move in a direction which runs perfectly parallel with the longitudinal axis of the body.

Underarms

Long with good muscles.

Middle Section of the Front Legs

Strong and short. Wrists are clean, smooth, without signs of *rachitis* (rickets).

The Front Paws (front limbs)

The bones are firm everywhere and the muscles are strong and not fleshy.

Feet

Quite round. The toes are bent and close together. The soles of the feet are thick and elastic. The nails are dark and strong.

Trunk

The trunk is robust without being plump. In the male dog, the length of the bow point to the end of the hipbone is approximately the same length as the distance from the top of the neck to the point where the neck meets the back. In the female dog, the length of this point may be slightly longer.

The Front of the Chest

Looking at it from the front, it is of medium width.

The Chest

Not very broad, but on the other hand, deep and low, like all animals with great endurance. The chest cavity is protected by ribs, which have to be arched at the top.

Schofthoogte

The highest point or angle of the shoulder has to be well-defined, with a clearly-drawn angle from neck to back.

Upper Line (back and lumbar region)

Straight, broad, and with solid muscles.

Belly

Moderately developed, not hanging down nor pulled up, with the underline lengthened with a flowing bow.

Crotch

Very lightly slanted, broad but without exaggeration.

Hind Legs (back limbs)

Strong, without being too heavy, and moving on the same level as the front limbs; they should stand perpendicular to the ground.

Thighs

Broad with strong muscles. The knees are located approximately perpendicular with the hips.

Shanks

Long, broad, and with muscles, and hooked sufficiently at the jump joints. However, without exaggeration, the jump joints (or ankles) are low to the ground, broad and well-muscled. Looking from behind, they should have the same width.

The Middle Part of the Hind Legs

Solid and short. Wolf claws are not desired.

Feet

Light oval. The toes are bent and well-closed. The soles are thick and elastic, with the nails dark and thick.

The Tail

The tail has been placed well, heavy at the start and of a medium length. While resting, the dog lets the tail hang, the end slightly turned towards the back at about the height of the ankles. When in movement, the dog raises the tail up; then the curve of the end is more defined, without forming a hook or an oddity.

The Coat

a. *Mask*: The mask has to give the impression that the upper and lower lips, the corners of the mouth and the eyelids are all included in this one black zone. Even with a light-colored coat, the mask has to be well-pronounced.

b. *Colors*: Dark red, black, flecked. The total color scheme goes from dark red to gray to black. A little white at the chest or the toes is allowed.

c. *Skin*: Elastic, but tight-fitting over the whole body. The outward membranes are strongly pigmented.

Size

The proper size is approximately 62 centimetres for male dogs and 58 centimetres for females. This is measured from the ground to the point where the neck is extended over the back (called the *schofthoogte* or highest point of the shoulder). The

"Robbie", a mixed Malinois, was for years a service dog with the Zaanstad Police Department.

allowable differences are 2 centimetres under and 4 centimetres above.

Movement

The movement is free and lively with the ability to cover terrain to a maximum. The Malinois is constantly moving and seems untiring. Because of his exuberant character, he has a definite tendency to go in circles instead of taking a straight line.

Faults

a. *Character*: Over-aggressive or timid.

b. *Nose, Lips and Eyelids*: loss of pigment.

c. *Teeth*: Light over- or under-bite.

d. *Eyes*: Light-colored.

e. *Shoulders*: Too straight.

f. *Hind legs*: Weak, ankle joints that are not sufficiently hooked.

g. *Feet*: Facing outward and separated.

Disqualifying Faults

The following mainly disqualify the dog for a pedigree, but if too serious, they can also disqualify a dog for police work.

a. *Teeth:* Definite over- or under-bite. Missing certain molars (missing small molar PM1, located right behind the eyeteeth, is allowed without penalty). However, missing two PM1s or missing another tooth similar to that molar will cost the dog his qualification. Also, the lack of three of these molars or two big teeth causes disqualification.

b. *Ears*: Hanging and manipulatable.

c. *Tail*: Born with short tail, or a tail shortened due to injury.

d. *Color*: White spots in other places than the chest and the toes. Lack of black mask.

e. *Character*: Must be approachable, with no hypertension or nervousness.

Sizes

Medium build male is 62 centimetres at shoulder height (*schofthoogte*).

Length of the Body
The chest to the end of the hip bones is 62 centimetres.

Length of the Back
From the neck (the *schoft*) to the comb of the pelvis is 41 centimetres.

Circumference of the Chest
Measured from behind the elbows, at least 75 centimetres.

"Zorro" with his handler. "Zorro" was also a mixed-breed Malinois.

The Depth of the Chest
    31 centimetres.

Length of the Head
    25 centimetres

Length of the Front Snout
    From 12.5 to 13 centimetres

Description of the Malinois

The hair on the head is very short, as it is on the outside of the ears and underside of the limbs. The hair is short on most of the rest of the body, fuller on the tail and around the neck, where a light collar is formed which starts at the base of the ears and spreads out to the throat. Also, the back side of the thighs has longer hair, which is called a fringe. The tail comes to a point at the end.

The mask must have a minimum of 8 pigment points: the two ears, the two upper eyelids, the upper and lower lips have to be black. Darker colors such as drab-reddish (fauve) are not acknowledged by breeders, but certainly do not affect the dog's ability to perform police work.

General Faults

Long hair, where it should be short; long hair distributed between the short; wavy hair. The lack of black streaks (charbonne) or the presence of spots. Not enough of a mask. Too much charbonne on the body is not desirable. Mating of hair varieties of the breed of the Belgian Shepherd is not allowed by the approving authority of the FCI (Federation Cynologique International).

3

The Dog and the Dog Handler

The Purchase

Before purchasing, you have to be certain that you *want* a dog. Of that, you have to be very *sure*. Owning a dog brings, of course, a few things with it that you cannot ignore, especially with the purchase of a Malinois. Usually we talk only of such things as letting the dog out, taking care of the animal, giving the necessary attention, in short, a hobby which takes a lot of time. If you are not absolutely sure you can do all these things, you are not ready for a Malinois. The entire family will be affected and must commit to caring for the new dog. However, if you still think you are ready for this, then you are ready to have a dog. My intention here is not to frighten you off from owning a Malinois, but I want people to be responsible in their dog ownership, and to draw your attention to the responsibilities involved *before* you purchase a dog.

A dog, whatever kind it is, is a living being. It cannot just be left to take care of itself. It needs care and attention. But if you are ready, then we are going to look for a suitable dog, particularly for a Malinois.

By the way, you should be equally sure, if you are a police officer, that you want to be a police dog handler. Please think long and hard about it, because that too is no small matter. I will write more on the subject later.

At this stage, let us assume it has been decided to buy a Malinois. The following information is then necessary.

a. Find a good breeder, or if you desire to have an older dog, find a private party whom you know well who has a dog for sale.

b. Ask questions about the pedigree and compare the tattoo number in the ear of the dog with the numbers on the pedigree, so you can be sure you are purchasing the dog that is named on the pedigree.

c. If the dog does not have a pedigree, then you must be more careful. Ask the seller, for instance, about previous litters and consult a veterinarian and ask if the given date of birth or the age is correct. An experienced veterinarian can determine a dog's age with considerable accuracy. Remember, most Malinois purchased for police work today do not have pedigrees.

d. Has the dog been dewormed and does he have the necessary inoculations? Ask for his inoculation booklet, in which you will find the age most of the time. Is it a pedigreed dog? Then you can compare the information to determine whether this is the same dog as the one the pedigree indicates. If the seller does not completely satisfy you, then do not buy the dog.

e. Inspect pedigreed dogs and look at the bloodlines. When you find among the list dogs with HD+ behind their names, which means they had hip dysplasia, do not buy this dog. Go over the pedigree and be critical. If you are concerned about an older dog, insist on a hip X-ray and let a veterinarian in your area look the dog over carefully. Do not be satisfied with an existing X-ray picture or other information about the dog.

f. Look again at the pedigree and see if there are titled dogs listed. This will give you a clue as to the dog's character and trainability. It's not absolutely necessary, but it will help give you a good idea of what your future friend is going to be like. You will have to educate the dog yourself for the most part, but if you have a chance to see the mother, do so. When the mother is a quiet, self-assured dog, it means that your young four-footed friend has most likely also inherited some of that self-esteem. With the older dog, you may want to take him right then and there and play some games, simple exercises which can show you what the dog is capable of.

g. Take along an experienced dog handler when you plan to purchase. It is one of the most important preventive measures you can take.

In short, make it just a little more difficult for the seller and tell him, for instance, at the beginning, that you wish to test the older dog and what you would like to see. Tell him what you plan to do, otherwise you may have difficulties during the testing. Be sure, however, that what you plan will give the dog an honest chance and don't expect it to perform impossible requests. The seller must also have an honest chance to sell his dog. There are plenty of good breeders out there, but it is a good idea for you to be somewhat educated.

If you are purchasing this dog to do more than just live in your home, there are two things you absolutely must test – the dog's courage or bitework, and his play- or prey-drives. When the dog you are interested in stands in front of you, having found a ball that you had hidden, with a questioning look as if to say, "When may I do this again?" then you are probably on the right track. But that is not all, because you also want to know if the dog will bite.

Most of the time, a dog has been offered to you and you want to try it out, first on the short distance and then on a greater distance. You can test his courage "by the stick and by the shot." Challenge the dog by throwing objects at him that cannot hurt him, and test his reaction to the sound of a gun being fired nearby.

Test the dog in the field and in a building, but absolutely not on his own terrain, because then you cannot be sure of the dog's capabilities. The dog has to show what it can do, or you may pay the price out in the field later. In the real world they do not ask questions. Something happens and you have to decide on a course of action, and you must be able to say that the dog and I have often met the challenge or crawled through the eye of the needle!

You should have an honest dog that will respond properly under all circumstances, that will be comfortable working when there are many people around, and that is completely trustworthy. A dog that has nothing to fear, combined with a boss who can stand up for himself, means the team provides support for each other. To be a team means more than having a good police dog and a good police dog handler.

Having an experienced handler with you when you shop for the dog ensures that attention is given to the combination by an experienced instructor, someone who has himself trained dogs, but does not have personal feelings for the dog in question. It has to be someone who really knows all the potential problems, but also one who can pass that knowledge on to others, who can get along with people, and who understands conflict and can explain potential problem situations.

In the dog world, it is very important to be able to deal with people and with conflicts, to handle them and to find solutions. Dog handlers are by nature very dominant people! The same holds for the helper (or decoy), who has to be an expert in his field. He really has to be able to help and he must know when to apply pressure and when to back off.

A good handler in the first phase of the training, coupled with a good helper, is the best situation. This ensures the dog can handle the training and that the dog is not overwhelmed by an inexperienced helper. Try to use the same helper throughout the initial training. The dog will be more comfortable and will learn much faster.

Which Sex? Which Malinois?

The choice of breed was not difficult. The choice of which sex is up to the new handler. I think a female dog is just as good as a male, as long as it is tested and chosen properly.

The female has the disadvantage of going into heat twice a year for three weeks and that can be a nuisance. They cannot be trained during that time because they cannot concentrate. It is also difficult to train male dogs if a female dog in the neighborhood is in heat. However, there is a medication for female dogs that can be used during that time so that the dog can continue training (available under various brand names; ask your vet for more details). However, most of the time preference is given to male dogs.

How old should such a dog be? In Holland, we take a pup when it's about 10 weeks old. We choose pups who have good parents, who have shown the capability for training, or parents who have already passed their training. Police officers wait for dogs that are a little older, so they can start training right away. They choose dogs, for instance, who already have a certificate KNPV 1, and who are eligible for the certificate of a service dog examination. Of course, there are also police officers who buy a younger dog and go into training with the objective of obtaining a police dog certificate.

In any case the dog, especially a police dog, should be an animal who shows that he knows what he is doing and when the handler asks, he will pay attention to everything and is afraid of nothing. Choose a good bright dog, one who likes to bite, paired with the necessary mentality and desire to work, and finally with a good social character and you have your best dog. Pick a dog with a personality you can enjoy, because you will spend a lot of time with your new partner.

The chosen dog is taken home and should be introduced to everyone there. A good dog is for the whole family and should also be capable of relating to others who take a liking to him or her. You do not want a dog that you have to keep away from everyone because you cannot trust him. The Malinois you have bought is such a dog – a dog who is ready to do anything for you if you want him to, and a dog who is screaming to be put to work of any kind.

Malinois female with puppies.

Which Malinois? The short answer is, *a good one* – one with talent and good characteristics – one who likes to work and sits in his kennel waiting for you – one who burns with the desire to work – one for whom you can throw a ball, which he will retrieve for you with delight, asking for more.

It's up to you to let him know that the games are a learning experience for his future work. But by then a few months have passed. By then you have a dog who loves people and things and one who keeps an eye on everything.

Throw a ball in the tall grass or in the brush and see if he looks for it and keeps on looking until the ball is found.

Go with the dog to a place where he has to look behind all sorts of obstacles to find his ball. Place the ball in a vice in such a way that it is difficult to retrieve and see how the dog works on it. It he gives up on it, then keep that in the back of your mind – later on it may assist you in deciding if you are going to keep this dog for training.

Throw his ball for him on slippery floors. In short, test the dog in all kinds of situations to make sure this is the dog for you. Maybe this is the dog you are waiting for and the dog is waiting for someone like you – a perfect match.

Also give thought to a dog who has already won one or more sporting certificates or competitions, but perhaps not enough for his former handler. This dog could perhaps be a good police dog. A real police dog is trained for fighting crime, not winning cups.

The Handler

The Malinois now has been chosen. It is logical that not all handlers belong with every dog. It really has to click between the handler and the dog, otherwise it will not work. The dog has to complete certain tasks, as does the handler, who must work with the dog. The discussion here is for *police* dog training, so first we must consider the police officer.

This police officer has to be good and ready to put out extra effort for the dog and the work. Experience in police work is also necessary.

Of course, the handler has to be an animal lover, especially a dog lover. To make a dog handler out of a police officer just because one thinks he is suitable for it is absolutely wrong. A police officer has to show why he thinks he is suitable to be a dog handler. He also has to know there are disadvantages in having a service dog. These dogs are bred and trained to be working animals, and therefore don't always make the best family pets.

A service dog is an excellent support, whatever kind of support is required – patrol dog, detector dog or dual purpose dog. A K9 team can be an excellent weapon in the fight against crime if the dog really is a good service dog and the handler is a fine, honest police officer.

It is important to understand that a dog, even if you have chosen him very carefully, and even in spite of his pedigree, can be a failure and this can be a big disappointment to you. Maybe your second or third dog will still not be the right one – you just never know! I know this sounds like a gloomy prospect, but you must know. But it is also possible that things will work out with your first dog, and you can all at once have a beautiful dog and make your name with your partner.

The dog, of course, is a living creature with his good and bad points, like a human being. The dog can sense your moods and feelings. You will have to make the dog subordinate to your will and make him clearly understand how you want him to obey. If you train the dog properly, he will demonstrate his subordinate position. The handler here takes the place of the leader in the dog world, the Alpha male of the pack.

It is very normal in the animal world for two or more of the dominant animals to fight for leadership. Such behavior some-times also appears in training and the dog can show dominant behavior toward the handler. That is the moment you must let him know who is boss – the handler, of course! By maneuvers, corrections and rewards, you can be in the dog's good graces, even if he has to be the subordinate one.

There are so many situations in which you can find your-self, and that variety is just what makes the training process so attractive. You may also find yourself in situations which you may not know how to handle. Let those exercises wait for a while before trying them again, but right away do another exercise whose outcome you know, so that you and the dog don't lose confidence and the dog knows its place. Later on, try to figure out what went wrong and try it again or ask another handler. Even the most experienced trainers make mistakes. Experience is very important, but doesn't cover everything. In the end, the dog will give an excellent performance, when he knows what expected of him. You and the dog will survive!

The dog is an objective animal. It doesn't make any difference to the dog whether he has to work on a murder case or if it is a very small case. He doesn't ask for reasons. If he has learned a task, he will work because he knows that he gives you great pleasure. He does it for you and nobody else. He is serving you! That is where he gets his *motivation*. To lay your will on the dog, in the most positive sense of the word, means that you need to have a balance of both physical and mental dominance over the dog's will. Sometimes you need physical strength, sometimes mental strength.

Every dog should be trained by means of the same method, but because every trainer and every dog are different, there will have to be some individualization. The amount of time it takes for you and the dog to learn to work together will vary. A long leash should be used by the trainer, even if the dog has already been trained and you are his second handler. With the long leash it is possible to tell the newly acquired service dog that he has to be attentive again and cannot do what he would like to do.

Before the Training

After the dog has been purchased we use, as I call it, the "walk and talk" method. This method is very simple to set up and is extremely important in the overall training. During this period, which lasts about 3 to 4 weeks, you simply take your new dog for walks for approximately an hour each day. During this walk ("walk"), the dog is being talked to ("talk") so that he can get used to your voice.

Here, of course, we are talking about a dog who, for the most part, has been trained. The dog will learn to trust you and will know that when he hears your voice, this is the voice of the boss. During this 3 or 4 week period, you are really training the dog, although the pressure from you on the dog is next to

Following ("Volg") on a leash.

nothing. Some pressure has to be there, though, so that the dog knows you are not there for nothing. The dog is always on the leash, so that he doesn't get the chance to goof off. The pressure gets increasingly more intensive, first by taking the dog out of the kennel and putting him in his rightful place at your left side by command. Hook the leash and order him to follow, after which you start walking and at the same time, with a short but strong jerk to the leash, let the dog know that he is to follow. The dog will know what this is all about and will cooperate to avoid the jerk on the leash. After about 10 or 12 steps, stop and give the command "Halt."

In the real world, the dog will have to walk through all kinds of situations, like loud noises, crowds, passing vehicles of every type, buildings and open areas, or light and dark areas. In short, let the dog experience as much as possible. The more varied the experiences you subject him to in the beginning, the better his response will be when working. It takes the older dog about 3 or 4 weeks in this period.

Sit for a while in a railway or bus station and let everything and everyone pass by you and the dog. If there is an airport in your area, let the dog walk on the slippery floors in the hallway with all those people, carts, wheelchairs, etc. Take a short train or bus ride with the dog. Let the dog go in and out of the train/bus. Make it clear to him, while talking to him, that everything is O.K.

Go with your dog up the stairs to the second floor of a building and then back down on the escalator, or the other way around. In short, look for as many situations as possible to which you can introduce the dog and keep a very close eye on how he reacts. By those reactions, you can learn much about the character of the dog.

With a pup, of course, this building up is totally different. With a pup the work will start very carefully. With younger dogs, from puppies to approximately a year old, you build them up with all kinds of new experiences. One of my most memorable experiences happened when I started with 4 puppies from the moment they were allowed to leave the litter. I took them all over the place in an effort to make them world-wise. It sure cured me. Each dog, of course, had its own character, which doomed my project from the beginning. At the end of the long road, I was disappointed. Not all the dogs did what I expected. Only one dog, Athos, ended up in police work and is now a police dog in Honolulu. The other three were fine house pets, but as police dogs, they lacked a lot.

Dogs who already have received police dog certificates sometimes show undesirable behavior, which does not bode well with how they will handle their task ahead. The dog in the hands of a new handler should be able to work in all kinds of situations and places. In order to reach that objective, he should have been just about any place and he should have retrieved and bitten in as many environments as possible, so that he doesn't hesitate when he suddenly finds himself in an unfamiliar building.

In the country where I am a proud inhabitant, there live and work many trainers who do not bother to look any further than the ends of their noses. They often train a dog according to the specific requirements of the certificate, but forget to take the time to work the dog through experiences he will have to cope with in his work life. When you buy a dog, you definitely have to look at all of these things. Otherwise you might, or perhaps I should say you will, find out later that you have been taken. Don't decide to buy a dog based only on a good search and bite exercise, but ask if the dog is capable of handling a lot more than that.

Using Malinois to guard the Feyenoord Stadium in Rotterdam.

The dogs that I recommend have to show what they are worth outside of the exercise terrain. Test their character in a shopping centre, in a railway station, at an airport, in a hallway on a slippery floor, etc. It helps a lot, although I am convinced that even later there may be some things which you did not expect. If you use my method, that chance is very small and you should remember that prevention is half the cure. My intention is to convince you that a dog has to be walked and talked to, giving yourself and the dog the opportunity to get to know one another. With this method, you "have killed two birds with one stone," namely you get to know one another better, but you also give the dog some other knowledge and a secure feeling in the places and with the things you expect him to handle in real life.

Obedience

Everything depends on a good general appearance, good obedience, together with the motivation of the dog and his desire to work. He must enjoy his work and accept the will of the handler gladly. This is why it is important that the two of you get along so well. The dog is not a tool that you can put in a closet after you use it. It is not a pistol, a truncheon or a motorbike. *No,* it is your partner, the living tool with whom you have to do a lot of work and on whom you can depend in many situations. The basis has been laid in the previous section "Walk and Talk" and now we have to go on. We have to build out and up.

With all due respect to the trainer in the sport dog world, there is a lot more to a *real police dog* that must be there naturally and through training.

We begin, if the dog hasn't learned this yet, by teaching him to lay down, sit up, bark on command, fetch and carry, if necessary even under pressure. Make an obedience exercise out of everything and give the dog opportunities to make mistakes, so that you have the chance to correct him. In short, be completely involved with the dog, so that he feels someone is paying attention to him.

Due to all this attention, the dog gets more and more joy in his work and his motivation grows because there is more direction in the training. Change activities as often as possible and make an exercise out of everything. Be quick to treat the dog if the exercise went well. It not only motivates your dog, but it also motivates you as the handler. Make an obedience exercise of the fact that you are letting him out of his bounds. Don't let him pull you to the place where he thinks he should leave his first scent mark.

Before you command a dog call his name, so he knows a few seconds before that he will receive a command, like *Halt,* etc. He hears your voice and is prepared to answer your command, whatever it is. There has to be a few seconds between calling his name and giving the command, because you have to give the dog time to react. You have to do this every time, because it has to become a habit for you and your dog.

Command the dog while he is still in the kennel by saying *Here,* open the door of the kennel immediately after that, and stand in such a way that the dog can pass you only on your right side (for the dog the left side) and give him the command *Plaats* (meaning on the left side of the handler, the head of the dog at his left knee), wait a moment and give him the next command *Volg* (which means follow me at the left side in the neighborhood of the left knee) and walk, "followed" by the dog at the left of you, to the spot where you think he should be let out and then give the command *Astor* . . . . *Halt,* and after that, *Astor* . . . . *Free.*

At the moment you give the command *Free,* have the dog on a longer leash of approximately 2 metres, but in such a way that when the dog has relieved himself you can command him immediately to his place in the same way you did when you let him out of the kennel. When the dog does that right, let him know with a couple of pats on his chest, while at the same time, with a glad voice, you give him your approval.

When everything goes according to plan, you can do a few exercises in between, such as giving the dog the command *Luid* (Loud) after which the dog is supposed to bark. Barking is necessary when searching for people and objects and it is good to let him know when barking is appropriate. The dog knows how to bark already, but he doesn't know the command. You can start to make it clear for the dog by raising one of your fingers, or be very active by touching a box every time with your fingers or your hand. Also act a bit busy, which will arouse the dog's natural curiousity and excitement. He will bark perhaps one time and then you give his reward. After a while, he will bark very well. Barking is a roll call exercise.

When training be sure to change activities once in a while. For instance, when the dog has done well, throw him a tennis ball to retrieve. Remember, let him fetch it and bring it to you. If the dog starts to play with the ball on his own and then lays down and bites on it, command him to return to you by calling *Astor* . . . . *Here* and at the same time, give your command a bit more power by giving a jerk on a leash of approximately 10 metres. The dog will come to you in a straight line and just before he is in front of you, pull him with the help of the leash around you and to your left side with the command *Plaats.* After that take the ball and throw it away for a short distance and that will make the dog very active, when he is a very good player.

You can also do this exercise in two parts and let the dog sit in front of you with the command *Astor . . . . Here*, show the ball and bring it around your body with the command *Plaats* and pull the dog with the help of the leash around you. As soon as he is there and sitting, throw the ball away a short distance as a reward. Next time and every time after that he will see this as a game he likes very much and he will work for you. When you are done, remember to command the dog to your left side, as indicated before, give him the command *Astor . . . . Volg* and then march away with him.

Get his attention by using his name and then give the command after about 3 to 4 seconds. When he is not paying sufficient attention, command his attention again by calling his name and then give a short jerk on the leash as a sort of correction. Don't forget this. Practice it yourself every time, because it is important. This is to show the dog that he cannot do what he likes. After you speak his name, the dog expects something from you. And this is not all. These exercises should come more often and in more diverse cases, and should finally become a second nature for you and the dog. At least that is what we hope for.

Perhaps you yourself are not teachable, but then we have to be honest with you and fair to the dog. Perhaps it would be better after all if you looked for another job or hobby.

When training a dog, there is a proper way to give a command to the dog. Don't ever yell at the dog. To give a command with a louder voice is alright, but that is different from yelling. The louder voice is positive, whereas yelling is negative to the dog. Give the command at the proper moment. This is especially important when you are correcting him. When the command or correction has not been given on the right moment, namely right after the moment of transgression or after you discover it, a fraction of a second and then the dog has lost the connection between the transgression and the correction, making that correction *worthless*. The dog has to learn to understand what he did not do right when you continue to correct him. Otherwise your corrections will be the start of a misunderstanding between you two and the dog will be confused. It will then, even though it may not be serious, take you days or weeks to undo the mistake you have made.

Challenge the dog to make mistakes and when he does, there is your chance to correct. When he is making a mistake, correct him with the command *Foei* or *No* (*Shame On You*) and give a jerk on the leash, too. Don't use the dog's name before the command, because it takes too long for the correction command.

Correcting with electric shock is something I do not recommend, because my impression is that most people do not know how to use it in the right way. That is why most of the time it looks like animal cruelty instead of proper correction, given at the right time and in the right way. Too many of these apparatus end up in the wrong hands!

See in every instance an opportunity for training and do not hesitate to create instances by which you can let your dog train.

Take care to take the dog's collar off with two hands, and never with one hand. Let the dog know you are careful. Taking the collar off with one hand can be painful for the dog, whereas it won't be if two hands are used. The understanding you have with your dog does not get better if you make these sloppy mistakes and hurt the dog unnecessarily.

Remember that giving more commands doesn't necessarily work. By constantly repeating your commands, you teach the dog to ignore them. The more commands the less they are worth. If the first command isn't followed, the second must be given with a tone of correction and maybe you want to add a little strength, without hurting the dog. For example, you may want to try the following method while training the dog to lay down. Take a large metal pin with an eye on one end and push it into the ground. Pull the leash through the eye of the pin and attach the leash to the choke chain of the dog. By the command *Astor . . . . Af* (Down) the dog is supposed to lay down. If he doesn't do that, then you use a command of correction by again using that command with a firmer tone and at the same time pull the leash tighter through the eye, so that the dog *has* to lay down. By this you let the dog know you won't accept his behavior and if he repeats it, you will absolutely pull him down. If the dog is doing well after that, he receives a treat.

We have been talking about yelling and loud commands. If the dog has progressed to the stage that he understands the commands, then also try talking to him with soft commands and with whispering. It has a practical value, for instance, if you are watching suspects and don't want them to know that you and your service dog are in the neighborhood and that they are about to come in contact with the dog in a very unpleasant way. In my experience, there have been many people whose lives we have made difficult in this way. It also has the benefit of helping to reinforce the bond between you and your dog.

Treats and Correction

I find this subject one of the most important parts in the training of the service dog. By means of treats and corrections, it is possible to teach the dog in training how to behave.

Concentrating on positive developments in the training of the dog, you will have to constantly treat him when he performs correctly or shows improvement. The reward only has to be the words of praise such as "How brave you are" or "That is a good boy," and the voice of the boss should be full of praise for that achievement.

In fact, the boss praises himself, too – after all, it is he, together with the dog, who performed. The reward has to be meant sincerely, because the dog knows real quick that he has been fooled and then his training backslides. Many up-and-coming dog handlers fail on this subject, because they cannot put real sincerity into it. With a reward, the handler really has to be spontaneous, and not everyone has that gift.

Of course, a reward is always the best thing you can do, while correction always is a bit sad. However, correcting is very important in the training of a service dog, because you impress something on the dog. In this particular case, because you don't want him to repeat bad or incorrect behavior.

By using the reward/correction system, the trainer helps the dog learn the difference between the correct and incorrect behavior, which most Malinois are able to figure out, I can assure you of that. Sometimes a handler leaves the correction or the reward undone, because he doesn't find it necessary. By failing to do that, you allow a tremendous opportunity to pass by to let the dog know what it was all about the first time. It is also important, of course, that the reward and the correction happen the moment after the dog worked well or when he made a mistake. The dog then learns the connection between when he has done something well or when he has done something badly.

In fact, a very big part of the training of the dog is built on that. Correction usually is done by using the words *No* or *Foei* (Shame) and then spoken in a punishing tone. The dog has to know by the sound of the voice that he was wrong and so any word used would be right, if done in that tone of voice.

The Team

As indicated before, obedience is a fundamental part of the total. But obedience has to be just a little more. Obedience has to be enjoyable, too, for the dog and his handler. The dog who enjoys his work will add that little bit extra to his performance.

In fact, the handler has to have the same thing. He or she also must want to work and also accept discipline. Correctness should not be a stranger to the K9 police officer, whose behavior should be consistent. However, honesty is also important. Someone who, as a trainer, has the correct dog in hand and thinks about his well-being, will go a long way. You can see them on the training field. Of some you can say, even though they haven't done much training yet, that they will not go far; while for others, it can be said that they are naturals, teams which, with a little guidance, can become quite something.

Some, because of a lack of knowledge, don't go far, but that is often because of a lack of commitment to a dog or a club. They have another dog every week and change from club to club because they cannot get along with either the dog or the club. Such people you are better off without in the dog world.

Only if the right ingredients are there, which in this case are a positive handler and a solid dog, can you speak of a combination that has something and from which something good can grow!

Equipment and Command Glossary

For training, the handler has to have certain items to help him. These items should be kept at or brought out to the exercise field for general use. The handler may wish to choose additional items for use in training his dog.

Some of the items the handler needs:

a. a short leash of approximately 1 to 1 1/2 metres;

b. a long leash of approximately 10 metres;

c. a fetch and carry block;

d. a number of small objects, such as keys, a wallet, some coins, some wooden articles, for searching;

e. a couple of large objects to retrieve;

f. a couple of steel pins with an eye;

g. some metal rods;

h. a solid rubber ball;

i. a slip chain; and

j. a broad leather collar.

Also on the exercise field there needs to be a bicycle with wheel covers (very important), a pistol, various large objects to retrieve, such as a chair, a crate, a bicycle wheel, a rifle, the tire of a car, etc.

On the field, there should be a ditch (2.25 metres across), a hedge (1 metre high) and a fence (1.75 metres high), constructed according to the requirements, and a couple of bite suits of various kinds to do exercises of various types.

Today there is the electric shock training device, which is being used whether or not it is suitable. I have to indicate to you that I have always been fortunate to be able to train dogs without this particular apparatus. To use it is O.K., but only instructed by people who know what they are doing. It is your own choice, but I will never use it!

Dutch Commands

Command	Pronunciation	Meaning
Braaf	Braaf	Good Dog
Hier	Here	Heel
Plaats	Plaats	Heel
Voet	Foot	Heel
Zit	Sit	Sit
Af	Af	Lie Down
Los	Losh	Release
Zoeken	Zooken	Seek
Vast . . . . Stellen	Fast/Shtellen	Get Him/Bite(?)
Let Op	Let Op	Watch Him
Revier	Revier (roll the r)	Area seek
Hoog	Hoog	Jump High
Breed	Breed	Jump Wide
Foei	Fooy	Stop It
Nee	Nee	No
Blijf	Blive	Stay
Volg	Folg	Walk Beside
Stil	Shtil	Be Quiet
Vry	Fry	Free to Go
Vast . . . . Apport	Fast/Apport	Hold Tight
Apport	Apport	Fetch, Retrieve
Uitkomen	Outkomin	Come Out
Luid	Lud	Loud (Bark)
Halt	Halt	Stop

German Commands

Command	Pronunciation	Meaning
Hier	Here	Come Here
Fuss	Foos	Heel
Sitz	Sit	Sit
Platz	Platz	Lie Down
Bleib	Blibe	Stay
Steh	Shtay	Stand Still
Aus	Ous	Come Out
Pass Auf	Pas Ouf	Watch Him
Stellen	Shtellen	Get Him
Gut Brav	Good Brav	Good Boy
Nein	Nine	No
Such	Sooch	Seek
Apport	Apport	Retrieve
Still	Shtil	Be Quiet

4

The KNPV Inspection Program

KNPV stands for, in Dutch, *Koninklijke Nederlandse Politiehond Vereninging*, which means, in English, Royal Dutch Police Dog Association. It was founded in 1907.

In the KNPV testing rules there are two sections whose significance you will appreciate when you are done testing. The two are "The way you show the dog and what kind of a combination you and your dog are" and "The general appeal" (obedience). The examiners, in my opinion, have done this in an effort to emphasize the combination of man and dog and I think that has been done correctly.

The KNPV Testing Program

When you succeed in purchasing a dog and that dog has a KNPV certificate and a report card of the inspectors, it will include a list of exercises, a few of which I will now explain.

The examination starts with Division 1, which contains the following exercises:

1. Heeling on the leash;
2. Heeling without the leash and going on command to the right and on command to the left;
3. Heeling next to the bicycle;
4. Down and stay without the handler;
5. Refusal of food;
6. Refusal of found food;
7. Being quiet;
8. An off-lead jump over a hedge 1 metre high;
9. An off-lead jump over a fence 1.75 metres high;

45

10. An off-lead jump across a hole in the ground which is 2.25 metres wide; and

11. Article search of small objects.

Division 2 consists of:

1. Swimming across a body of water; and

2. Fetching a large object out of the water and bringing it.

Division 3 consists of:

1. Guarding an object;

2. Field search for a larger object;

3. Field search for a person;

4. Transporting a suspect;

5. Apprehending a helper armed with a stick;

6. Refusing commands of a suspect;

7. Transporting a suspect and apprehending him when he tries to escape;

8. Apprehending a suspect who is trying to escape on a bicycle;

9. Transporting a suspect, followed by guarding him;

10. Apprehending a man who is firing a weapon;

11. Apprehending a man who is throwing articles at the dog to hurt him;

12. Transporting the suspect and defending the handler when the suspect tries to attack him; and

13. Calling back the dog while he is chasing the suspect.

An extra exercise that is sometimes used is the false attack of the helper, who stands still, demanding that the dog not attack.

Such testing is completed with the judging of dog and handler, which is called "General Appeal" and "What kind of a combination you are, as a dog and a dog handler." The exercises to test the dog are judged using a scale from 0 to 5, and for the two sections that judge the team, a scale of 0 to 10 is used.

Do not think that this is the order of training, or is the order in which the dog has to be trained. Every dog differs in character and temperament and every handler is also not the same. That is why one should always allow for some differences in training.

Besides training with the training club, it will be necessary to train on the training fields of your service dog unit. Training at different places and at different times is a must, so that the dog gets used to working in different places and not just one type of area.

As I mentioned earlier, there can never be enough places to let the dog work to round out his training and experience levels. A dog that has been subjected to as many stimuli as possible will be there wherever and whenever he is needed. One of my habits is to test the dog outside of his training field with the thought that, in practice, the training field can be anywhere.

Of course, it is very nice to be able to show all kinds of trophies in the living room, which have been won at various competitions, but the most important thing for a police officer is how well his dog works in real life. That is why, as much as possible, his training has to be done in real life situations.

Keep a close eye on the dog's behavior, appraise it and adjust your training accordingly. If you can't appraise it, then talk to your instructor, who should be glad to help. Exchange ideas. A good instructor will be interested in what you have to say. *Two* know more than one. Of course, it is not possible or even necessary to share everything. There are solutions you can think of right there and then, which are adequate and should be used. The good and experienced handler often comes to his own conclusions and acts as his own instructor.

Take your time with training and don't train too long with one exercise. Be flexible and change over to other ones, so that training continues to be enjoyable, not only for yourself, but also for the dog.

Division 1 of the KNPV Inspection Program

First, there are the *follow exercises*, which consist of three sections, namely:

1. Heeling on the leash;
2. Heeling without the leash, and going on command to the right and on command to the left again; and

3. Heeling next to the bicycle.

1. Heeling on the Leash

The dog has a normal collar and a normal leash. The dog takes his place on the right or the left side of the handler close to the area of the knee. The handler commands *Astor . . . . Volg* and after that walks at a normal pace in one direction, as indicated by a task master. You have to be able to see there is some slack in the leash, while the dog continually walks next to the knee of the handler. I advise you to hold the leash with both hands during testing as well as training, especially not only with the hand which is the farthest removed from the dog. Correcting the dog works better with two hands. Does the dog work really well? Then you can give the leash a little more slack with the hand which is closest to the dog. When the dog makes a mistake, you can immediately make use of this hand in giving correction.

If you think the dog does good work, then let him know; do the same, of course, when he makes a mistake. You should be aware

Patrol work in a park with the dog following at the left side of the handler – note the slack in the leash.

that this is taking place in a bit of military style. As soon as you start jogging, the dog will do the same. Make definite movements toward the left and the right constantly, putting your knee against the dog with the left turn, but watch out that he doesn't start dancing in front of you. While doing a right turn, you should all of a sudden give a good jerk on the leash, which will make the dog watch you carefully when turning to the left as well as to the right. There is also "the turnabout" movement. All of a sudden, make a 180 degree turn and go back on your own tracks. It's best to choose a moment when the dog is not watching you carefully, then you can catch him off guard – correct him with a correcting movement and your correction command, *Volg*.

If you think that you are ready for another exercise, then command, *Astor . . . . Halt.* Wait approximately the length of two paces between the name of the dog and the command *Halt.* After stopping, the dog is supposed to sit next to you, waiting for things to come. During the following exercise, make certain that the dog never knows exactly which exercise or movement is coming up next. With this, you ensure that the exercise is not the same every time and you will increase the dog's awareness of you and your movements.

2. Heeling Without the Leash

This following exercise is to a considerable degree the

Heeling without a leash.

same as on the leash. If the dog has no difficulty with the exercises on the leash, he should be able to do them off the leash.

The dog gets the command *Astor* . . . . *Plaats* and takes his place at the right or the left hand side of the handler. It is usual to take the dog on the left side, but the other side is allowed.

The handler loosens the dog (takes off his collar and leash) and gives the command *Astor* . . . . *Volg*, after which, in the same way as if he were on the leash, they start to walk. While following without a leash, the inspector will sign the handler to give the command *Right* and *Left*, at which times the dog on command will go behind your back to your right and then back to your left side again. Command *Astor* . . . . *Right* (or *Left*), depending on which side the dog is on at the time. After this follows the same exercise, except in the opposite direction.

3. Heeling Next to the Bicycle

Following next to the bicycle is a little outdated, but still a very necessary exercise. A bicycle is leaning against a tree and you head towards it, followed by your dog on the leash (you must have started with the exercise "following on the leash"). A couple of metres before the bicycle, command the dog to *Halt* and remove the dog's collar and leash. Then walk without a leash to the bicycle. Just before reaching the bicycle, command your dog to the right at the same time as you take the bicycle away from the tree, so that you are on the left and the dog is on the right side, with the result that the bicycle is between you and the dog. Command the dog *Astor* . . . . *Sit* and, shortly after that, *Volg* and walk with the bicycle and the dog. Then jump on the bicycle and ride away.

Here, of course, it is also important that you don't always travel the same pattern, but rather a variety of patterns, so that the dog will give more attention to the handler. It goes without saying that you should correct or reward the dog accordingly during training. Correcting and rewarding during testing is not allowed (the result will be a deduction of points). When following the bicycle, the dog should walk on the right side, so that he is better protected from the traffic coming from behind.

4. Stay Down (Without the Handler)

After the following the bicycle exercise has taken place, the dog is shown a spot where he has to lay down. The handler commands the dog to lay down (*Astor . . . . Af*) and then to stay (*Blijf*), after which he walks away in a certain direction. The dog must stay in the laying down position approximately three minutes. Crawling, sitting up or standing leads to a lower score, and in the case of the dog getting up and walking away, a score of zero. After those 3 minutes, the handler gets another sign to get the dog.

You must test this after the dog has learned what *Af* (Down) is. The long leash is used and attached to the dog. The leash has been pulled through the eye of a stake which has been pushed in the ground. Remove yourself from the dog a little ways, in any direction; the dog will get a little restless, because he thinks you may leave him alone. The dog will try to stand, and you must immediately give him correcting commands, *Af* and *Blijf*, one right after another, while giving a jerk on the leash, pulling the dog down. Eventually the idea enters the dog's head that all he has to do is what you told him to do and he will be rewarded with a "Good Boy" or something like that.

You can build up the exercise by removing yourself farther from the dog. For that you can lengthen the leash a little so that you still have the dog under control and can correct if necessary. As long as the dog wants to stand up, etc., then continue to exercise on a shorter distance, or even go backwards a step. Don't be ashamed of having to take that step back. Many good results have come from that and this is better than continuing to fail at a longer distance.

You make sure the wind blows to the dog, so that he winds your presence in the area and knows you are still close enough to administer correction. When he does well and this is repeated many times, repeat it again by leaving the area completely. The dog has to be able to perform the task. By now it is not necessary to say that when the dog does the exercise well, you have to reward him. But again, take all precautions during training in this exercise. Let the dog know what is definitely not allowed, but do it in a responsible way, so that the dog enjoys his training times and knows the consequences of desirable and undesirable habits.

When the exercise is completed, walk to the dog. Do not walk too fast, but go directly to the dog. Stand next to the dog and give the command *Astor . . . . Plaats;* the dog will stand next to you and you reward him. Then give the command *Astor . . . .*

"Athos" during the lay down and stay for 10 minutes.

Volg and as he follows you, leave the field and go to a place where you can let the dog loose. Once there, stop with the familiar command *Halt* and after that, *Astor* . . . . *Vry,* which means free to go, giving him the opportunity to relieve himself, and now you can play with a ball with him. The command *Vrij* will also mean to the dog that he cannot always do what he wants to do, but only when he gets the command. Always let him know that clearly and keep yourself to that. It will benefit you and the dog as well.

5. The Refusal of Food

From a real-life safety perspective, you should train your dog to refuse food offered by anyone other than yourself or a family member. This will help prevent his being poisoned, whether deliberately or by accident, and will also prevent his being distracted from the pursuit of his task, which is to help capture criminals. It is also important that while the dog refuses the food he also bark madly at the person who offers the food to him. In testing, this so-called angry barking and the refusal of food leads to a high score.

6. The Refusal of Found Food

During the jumping and staying exercises, there should be a certain amount of food spread around by the wall, in a hole, or a container with food left in the hedge. This should also be done during the exercise of following the handler. You can imagine, this is a very difficult exercise for the dog and will have to be built up with the necessary care. To correct with too much force does not make sense. This exercise needs to be built up as much as the previous ones. Arrange for all the exercises where the refusal of food comes in to be practiced completely, so the dog is comfortable with it. Not until you and your instructor are satisfied with the progress of the other exercises can food refusal exercises be started. Practice this subject in all kinds of positive ways. Even have the dog lay next to the food, making it very clear to him that he is not allowed to have it. Do the jump exercises on the long leash, with a bowl of food placed near the obstacles. Given the difficulty of this task for the dog, be sure to reward and correct the dog in a responsible way, not by yelling at the dog and definitely not by hitting the dog.

Bring variations into this and don't train the dog in such a way that when he comes to the exercise field, he associates it with correction, "Here we go again." Always doing the same things and always in the same order is not very pleasant for you or the dog. Don't train on the exercise field only, but also in the city, in the train station, or in the open marketplace, etc., and be sure to let him know that you are glad when it goes well. You have probably seen the dogs that always go straight from the exercise field, hop in the carrier and after that the other way around back to the kennels behind the house. A dog who has exercised in a wide variety of locations and under different circumstances is worth a lot more. He has also a lot more to give. The difference is easily seen!

7. Being Quiet

This is also an obedience exercise by which you get the opportunity to lay your will on the dog, make him more manageable, especially in real-life situations, where it is absolutely essential that neither the dog nor you be detected.

A place will be assigned to you, where the dog is not allowed to bark, whine or manifest himself in such a way that it can be heard at a distance of 20 metres. You will be hidden in overgrown terrain, behind a fence or a building, etc., and the dog may lay, sit or stand during the exercise. The dog may be on a leash, but during testing, the dog should not be allowed to pull at or stretch the leash. It is the choice of the handler to take part in this exercise with the dog on-leash or off-leash. When the handler chooses off-leash and collar, he is allowed to put the flat of his hand on the dog's back, without pressing the dog to stay down during the noise of a shot from a pistol and the yelling of a judge.

Here again, the exercise has to be built up slowly to the level to which the dog must perform.

Someone will yell from quite a distance, and when that does not give any problems, someone will shoot. You have to try to keep the dog quiet. Talk to the dog in a peaceful, calm tone of voice. At the moment that he whines or tries to bark, immediately correct with the command, *Still* (Quiet). Get up from your squatting position, walk in a small circle with the dog while under obedience, and try again to do the same exercise in a different place.

I do not have to tell you that when the dog does really well, he should get a tremendous reward.

Jumping Exercises

In the inspection orders of KNPV there are three types of jumps:

8. The off-lead jump over a hedge 1 metre high;
9. The off-lead jump over a fence 1.75 metres high; and
10. The off-lead jump over a hole or a ditch 2.25 metres wide.

These jumping exercises start very simply, namely by creating or looking for small obstacles. You yourself should jump over the obstacles with the dog, with the command *Astor .... Hoog* (high) or *Breed* (broad), depending on the jump. After awhile it is not necessary to jump together with the dog. The dog now enjoys the obstacles and does not need the extra support. He can do it himself! There are some conditions connected to that jumping: the dog should be at least one year old and know all the general rules of obedience. After that, a jumping exercise goes continually higher or wider until the requirements of height and width have been reached.

"Zorro" jumping over a 1.75m fence. At the left is the author, without glasses and 15 years younger.

It is then required that the dog lay down, sit or stand on the other side. A jumping exercise goes as follows: at a distance of about 10 metres (as the dog becomes more comfortable with the exercise, increase the distance to 25 metres), the handler starts walking in the direction of the obstacle that has to be jumped. Upon arrival at one of the three obstacles, command the dog *Astor . . . Halt*, at which point you and the dog should be exactly at the same place so that you can give the jumping exercise a good chance of being correct. At a signal from someone (at the testing it is the inspector) you command *Astor . . . . Hoog* or *Breed*, depending upon which obstacle must be jumped. The dog jumps, and almost at the same moment, because the dog is moving so fast, you give the dog the command *Astor . . . Af, Sit* or *Blijf*, depending on what you want from him at the other side of the obstacle. It is important that once you have decided on a command, you stay with that command and don't change it.

In training for these obstacles, have a second person assist you, with a second long leash, stationed on the far side of the obstacle. The jump back, as well as the jump forward, can be controlled by these long leashes. The return jump is easier to control when a second line or leash is used by a second person. For the jump back, you have to give the command *Astor . . . . Here.* Quite often, it's too much for the dog to wait for the command and you will find that the dog is already on his way back before you know it. The dog ignores the command *Here.* To prevent that, you need that second person with the long line. When the name of the dog is called out for the jump back and the dog indicates that he will come before the command is given, the second person reacts by restraining the dog and gives a correcting command, *Blijf.* The combination of the intervention and the command make the dog realize that he is too early and soon he will find out what you really mean. It is not as difficult as it seems, but it does take some patience and concentration and with an extra handler, it is easier than by oneself.

At an inspection, the height of a hedge is 1 metre, the fence is 1.75 metres high and 1.25 metres wide. The hole or ditch is 2.25 metres wide, at least 3 metres long and 1 metre deep.

I would suggest you build the fence out of planks, leaving some open spaces so that you can see and control the dog and see that he has done your command for the jump forward (*Af, Sit* or *Stay*) and the jump back (not too early). If that is not the case, the dog needs a correction command.

11. Article Search

This section demands, as a very important component, a strong will to search and retrieve. Without this ingredient it will not work.

In the first place, the dog must be willing to pick up and hold in his mouth objects which it might otherwise never pick up, and so training might involve some coercion on the dog to pick up and bring the article. When the dog is compelled, you can be sure that when the dog finds the article by using his nose, he will pick it up and bring it. Not every dog is happy with holding iron or metal articles in his mouth, which are very hard. The dog is then made to take the article in his mouth under the command *Vast Apport* (hold tight), although the dog will not understand the words themselves. You have to make it clear to the dog by opening his mouth and placing the article in his mouth with the command to hold it.

As long as the dog keeps the object in his mouth, he will be "A good boy," and when he tries to drop it, give a correction command like *No, Vast* (which is "No, Keep It"), and after some time, again, he will understand what is expected of him.

It is also a requirement that the dog let go of the article on the command *Astor . . . . Los* (which means "loose"). So practice *Astor . . . . Vast* (the dog has to take it) and *Astor . . . . Los* (the dog has to leave it). With this you lay the basis for the bite work which comes later.

If the dog does not open his mouth when you take the object in your hands, you should squeeze his upper lip a little against his teeth. Repeat this when the dog will not let go of the article. We always try to ensure that the article does not fall on the ground. The article has to stay in the mouth of the dog and he has to offer it to the handler on command. When I begin this exercise, I usually use a metal pipe so that the dog gets used to metal right away. When the dog understands what is expected of him, then it is time to offer him the article half way from his mouth to the ground. At the same time we give the command *Vast*. When after several days the dog has done well, we change and place the article on the ground approximately 1 metre in front of the dog. The dog is, of course, on the long leash and we command *Astor . . . . Vast . . . . Apport*, after which the dog should jump forward, take the article from the ground, come back to you, sit in front of you and offer the article to you. After that he gets the command *Astor . . . . Plaats*, and with the help of that same long leash, he goes around you to take his position on your left side, with his head in the general area of your knee.

The time has now come to teach the dog to search for the article, since he now has retrieved the article when it is laid down further away from him. The articles in the next few weeks get smaller and are laid down on a piece of ground approximately 14 by 14 metres, grown over with grass. At first you do this yourself and later you should obtain some assistance from others, so that the dog gets used to seeking objects that have a stranger's scent, because at the inspection you may not lay the articles down yourself.

The articles are small, such as a bullet casing, keys, a button, etc., and not only made of metal. Wood, leather and plastic objects are used here. The dog should not be allowed to chew on the object. Chewing can result in the object being destroyed or damaged and that is not the intention. In a police investigation, the article can be evidence. The best thing is to teach the dog not to chew when you are teaching him to hold the object. Every time he tries to chew on the object, try to stop it right away with the command *Nee, Niet Bijten* (No, Don't Bite) as you hold the upper and lower jaws with both hands. During the search, you will notice that the dog catches the scent of the article from a distance. When you are training the dog, encourage him by talking to him softly and saying *Good Boy .... Zoeken* (Seek), and if the dog is not searching, give him the correction command, such as *Nee, Zoeken* (No, Seek).

When hiding the articles in the grass, make it a little easier for the dog in the beginning by giving him lots of easy clues. With objects in your hand, walk on to the field from a certain place. When you come to the spot you have picked out as the place where you want to hide the object, wipe your feet over the grass so that your scent is left behind on that spot, and the vegetation is a bit damaged. On that spot, place an article. From there, walk back to the point where you began and pick another article to drop at another spot and, just as with the first place, drop the article after you have wiped your feet. Repeat what you have done before for a third article. Return to the beginning point over the same path and pick up the dog, taking him along to a spot approximately 1 metre from the beginning point. Always take care, especially in the beginning, to have the wind in your face so that the dog has to search against the wind. At first, always use the long leash. Sometimes this is quite cumbersome, but as the weeks go by you will become handier with working with this long line. Take care there are no obstacles, like little trees or something else, in the field, because then the long line can get stuck and pull tight, making the dog think right away that he is being corrected and he doesn't know why. Such things work against the handler and dog and it takes some effort to get the dog on the right track again. Search from object to object, do not go back to the beginning point every time. The dog has to then, after finding the first article, on his own without help, trace the scent which leads to the second or third article. After a while, throw the articles to certain places in the field, first when the dog can see it and later when he is in your trailer or car and cannot see you throwing them. Take care to know where the articles are so that you can encourage your dog by praising him, and avoid correcting.

Finally, get a helper to throw the articles in the field while you and your dog are out of sight and do not know where the articles have been hidden. Now the dog must also search for a strange scent. At first, make sure there is enough scent on the articles, and later as the dog's skill increases, you can leave less scent by keeping the articles in hand for a shorter time. If that is going well, and changing the field doesn't bother the dog, then as far as this exercise goes, the dog is about ready. Except for getting a certificate, the dog is ready for a scenario in which a suspect tries to throw away an article he used, such as a knife, a key, a wallet, etc., in the tall grass, when police officers are trying to arrest him. Various police officers have been looking for it, but cannot find it. A police dog nearby can give his assistance, but you have to remember this has to happen as soon as possible.

The dog is thus trained on fresh scent. With this in mind, the dog handler has an opportunity to prove himself and the dog, ending on a positive note.

The search field should not be marked with all kinds of flags, poles or whatever, which were in the ground shortly before the exercise was to start. This is a mistake because fresh human scent is on these objects, which can completely confuse the dog. We cannot smell it, but the dog certainly can and could be distracted by it. You can mark a search field better by a distance between, for instance, two trees, two lanterns, or something like that. For this exercise, it is constantly explained to the handler where the borders of the field are. Do not forget the basis of the exercise and practice the commands *Vast* and *Los*.

So, now we have the first part of the KNPV program behind us. You will notice this is not a definitive manual which, for every combination of man and dog, guarantees success. These are only guidelines to get you started, and each handler and certainly the instructor, too, has to tailor the dog's and the handler's training to potential situations which could arise in their locale, with the help of the information in this book.

Division II of the KNPV Order of Inspection

This section contains the "Waterwork" and fetching exercises.

Division II has two parts:

1. Swimming across a body of water on command; and

2. Retrieving an object from the water.

To carry out these exercises you will need:

• a body of water a minimum of 15 metres long and a maximum of 30 metres wide;

• a body of water which is not dirty; and

• the water has to have a moderate temperature.

It is, of course, very clear, but I will say it anyway, that the dog has to have been inoculated against any contagious diseases.

There are two parts in this exercise – the dog must follow a command to swim, and he must do so in the specified speed and direction.

The dog has to swim across this body of water of at least 15 metres and, on command of the handler, has to lay down, sit or stand on the other side. The command for this can be the same as the jump exercises. The intention is that the dog stays as long as possible, or sits or stands until the handler gives the command. For the swim exercise the command *Astor . . . . Over* is used. The dog is brought to a certain point near the water and his handler sends him to the other side with that command. When the dog has completed his swim and returned to the shore, the command *Astor . . . . Plaats* is given, after which you, followed by the dog, leave the shore.

After this follows the exercise of bringing a large object back to the shore, where the handler is waiting. The object, usually a piece of wood, is thrown into the water, and you head, followed by the dog, to the edge of the water. At approximately a metre and a half from the edge of the water, the dog is given the command *Astor . . . . Halt*. Then the dog gets the command *Astor . . . . Vast* and he has to get the object floating about 7 metres away from the edge and bring it to his handler at the shore. After he has laid the object on the edge, he again gets the command *Plaats*, and then the handler leaves with his dog.

A dog who knows what it is to swim and really knows how to retrieve should not have any problem with this exercise. The dog gets the opportunity for retrieving from the water only after he has completed the exercise of swimming across.

When training the dog to swim across, always use the long leash, which has to be a little longer than the width of the water. The person who helps you has to have a long leash, too, and go stand on the other side of the water. After the command is given, the helper pulls the dog into the water and to the other side where he must lay, sit or stand until the handler gets his turn to pull the dog back to his place. Repeat it and repeat it in good co-operation with the helper. The dog handler and the helper keep the leash very tight to press the dog to go straight from edge to edge. Later on, the dog will swim straight to the other side and back without the leash, which he must do to complete the inspection program. It is also possible to use a steel pin on the other side of the water and work without a helper, but I recommend using a helper.

After a while, if everything goes well, most dogs will enjoy getting in the water so much that, in a manner of speaking, they are in the water before you notice it. Most dogs find it great. When the dog does everything well in the training area, then also go to other places, where, of course, the conditions I mentioned earlier are present. Some dogs love the water so much that I have seen them go into the water when they were not meant to, namely during the bitework exercises, and it was very difficult to get them out. The exercises have to be done in such a way that the dog understands that he can swim only when the handler allows him and gives the command.

Bite Work

Before proceeding into Division III of the inspection order of the KNPV, you have to be convinced that your dog bites well. You must test that with the help of an assistant when you purchase the dog. The dog has to have the courage to bite. Biting out of fear doesn't enter in here. I go on with the understanding that you have purchased a dog that you want to build up further as a good dog in training, but certainly not one who doesn't have the basic skills to succeed. Give the dog a couple of opportunities to bite. Some dogs are slow starters and later on improve quite rapidly.

The dog is by nature a biter, which means that you really do not have to teach him to bite, because a dog has always needed to bite in order to catch his prey and survive. Because of this, the dog can be a dangerous animal. From the time of pursuit to the seizing of the prey, everything is allowed, but at the moment the prey (helper) shows that he has given up, the biting is done. If things go well, the helper gives up his fight against the dog because he sees that the dog has the upper hand. A dog who needs further practice with biting must learn to win, in a certain way, and so you should let the dog win the fight between him and the helper. The more we give the dog the impression that he can win, the better he will bite and the better he will eat into the offered prey, namely the arm or the leg of the helper.

The handler also plays a very important role, as does the helper. Each one in his own way contributes to the growth of the dog. Both have to feel what is going on. The handler must encourage the dog by speaking softly to him, stroking him and rewarding him when he enthusiastically tries to seize his prey. The helper helps by letting the dog know that a person cannot stand against him.

Refusing commands from strangers, the shot, the stick and the throwing of objects exercises come later on, when the dog has a better understanding of what he is supposed to do. We first deal with building up the bite. At a much later stage, we will work on refining the bite, by using the exercises already discussed, and also by slowly increasing the distance between the handler and the helper. By increasing the distance gradually, you get a good picture of how the dog should be able to work. While in earlier years, beauty was most important, now attention is also placed on the strength of character. Those who breed beauties have to watch this, because a dog who is unsure of himself is not worth having.

As indicated before when I discussed carrying, which of course also means seizing prey, the commands "vast" and "los" are of great importance. The reward and correction are also, and I cannot say this often enough, very, very important.

It is preferable that the dog seize the legs. Seizing the legs gives the dog more security than biting the arm. There are no regulations regarding where the dog should bite, but the leg is seen as the safest. When the decoy is riding a bicycle, the leg is also the first choice.

The picture shows the police dog Robby, of the Zaanstad Police Department, during an examination. By seizing the arm, while attacking the rider of a bicycle, the dog's weight can pull down the helper, before he knows what is going on, to the ground, with the possibility that the helper and the bicycle could fall on the dog. This can upset the dog very much and it also can hurt the dog as well as the helper.

You have to start the bite work on the bicycle with the helper stopped with both legs on the ground and build it up to real cycling. Every time you work with the bicycle, you have to be careful and give the dog the opportunity to do his bite work, first from a very short distance and later on further and further away. Every time the helper has to lay down the bicycle very carefully and walk further with the dog still biting his leg. The dog is still working on a long leash at that time. This is the safest way to teach the dog to bite the helper on a bicycle.

Division III of the KNPV Inspection Program

Know the following exercises:

1. guarding an object;
2. retrieving/searching for a large object;
3. retrieving/searching for a person;
4. transporting a suspect;
5. stopping a person who is armed with a stick;
6. refusing the commands of strangers;
7. transporting a suspect and stopping him when he tries to escape;
8. stopping a suspect who is trying to escape on a bicycle;
9. transporting a suspect, followed by guarding him;
10. stopping a suspect who is armed with a gun and who shoots at the handler and his dog;

"Robby" chasing a decoy on a bicycle, as is usual in KNPV testing in the Netherlands. This was during a trial of the handlers in my dog unit in Zaanstad.

11. stopping a suspect who is throwing articles at the dog to distract him while the dog was stopping and guarding the suspect;

12. transporting the suspect and defending the handler when the suspect tries to attack the handler; and

13. calling back the dog when he was sent after the suspect.

These are the things which have to be accomplished during an examination with your dog and I now will explain the meaning of these and how to train for them.

1. Guarding An Object

This is judged in two segments, namely:

a. the way of guarding; and

b. the alertness of the dog.

The dog, in this exercise, has to finish the exercise himself, which means he cannot count on the help of his handler. The handler is out of sight. The dog guards an object chosen by the handler, which has been approved for testing.

The dog should have learned by now to stay down, *Vast* and *Los*, and the biting exercises. Now he is made to lay down next to an object and he has to stay there. During training, the handler at first stays with the dog, while the helper comes closer.

The dog will try to leave his place to bite the helper. The helper is not totally a stranger for the dog, because the helper was there from the beginning, when the dog was purchased and because you've been training him to bite the helper. With the help of a long leash, the dog has to learn to stay in one place, namely with the object he has to guard. The pin in the ground will help you, while standing behind the dog, to keep the dog in his place – the same way you did when you were training him to lay down.

Eventually the dog will understand that he has to stay until the helper comes within a certain distance of the guarded object and that only then can he start to attack. It is good idea to have the helper vary his approach to the object by walking alongside the object, standing still all of a sudden, and continuing to walk and increasing his pace. Constantly test the dog to see if he will stay down and to make it clear to him that he may only leave when the helper comes within that certain distance. When the dog successfully guards the object, the helper walks away, followed by the dog until he is so far removed from the object that the dog has to return to guard it again. You may, during training, have to order the dog *Los* and pull him back by the leash to the object he is supposed to be guarding.

By constantly repeating that exercise, the dog has it imprinted in his mind and eventually will not cause any problems. It is, of course, clear that the dog at certain times has to be rewarded or corrected, whenever necessary. As the dog becomes more familiar with the aim of the exercise, slowly increase the space between the dog (and the object he is guarding) and you, depending on how things are going and how the dog is learning. Until you have complete confidence that your dog can do the exercise, you should continue to control him with the long leash and correct him when necessary.

We continue with the retrieving exercise, namely the retrieving of a large object and the retrieving of a person.

2. Retrieving/Searching for a Large Object

This consists of the following sections:

a. waiting and following up the commands;

b. the way of retrieving;

c. barking;

d. guarding the object; and

e. not biting the object.

Retrieving means in fact searching on a larger piece of terrain, for example, four soccer fields. It actually can be compared with searching for small objects. In this instance, however, the area the dog must search is much broader in order to adequately hide larger objects, such as a motorcycle, a strong box, a rifle, a crowbar, etc., that is, an object which the dog cannot bring in, but must bark at. The five sections are critically judged in testing, so it's important that the dog learn to perform these tasks independently.

The command for retrieving of a large object is *Astor* . . . . *Retrieve* (or *Revier*), which most of the time is abbreviated to "RRRRRRRRR."

The handler takes the dog along to the edge of the area where the object is hidden and commands the dog to *Halt*, after which he presents himself to the inspector, who will tell the handler what is expected of him. The handler then gives the command to *Revier*, and the dog starts out and, if everything goes well, will bark when he has found the large object. After this the handler, on a signal from the inspector, or when in training from the instructor, walks along in the direction, together with the inspector or the instructor, of the barking dog. The dog will be judged for his barking on the way to the object and after that for his guarding. Upon a signal from the inspector the dog can be taken away. The handler rewards his dog and goes, followed by his dog, to the next staging area.

Before trying this exercise, you have to be sure the dog can bark well and at the appropriate times. Make use of every opportunity to teach the dog to bark – for his feeding, for letting him out, when bringing him back to the kennel, etc. Then apply that training selectively in such a way that you do not let the dog bark for every exercise. If you do, after awhile you have a dog that is barking against everything. You have a tremendous barker and that is not what we are looking for. When the dog has understood the command *Astor . . . . Loud,* we introduce a wooden crate and agitate the dog, bringing the crate to his attention by hitting it with the hand or with a stick. It will motivate good dogs to bark, because he already knows what barking is. Move the crate away over a short distance and send or bring the dog to the crate on a long leash and see what he does. If the dog starts to bark on his own, that of course is wonderful and you will be elated. If the dog does not bark right away, then get him to bark by letting someone else hold the leash while you walk to the crate and motivate the dog again by hitting the crate. Stay there each time if the dog does not bark and let him know that he has to bark. Start moving again as soon as the dog barks and stop again if he does not bark, so that eventually the dog understands that he is not doing one step when he is not barking. There are thousands of varieties possible, but you strengthen the exercise by moving the crate a little further away. While you are walking away you constantly let the dog see the crate and knock on it. The dog will definitely get a taste for it.

When you come back, attach the dog to a long leash, but make sure that this long leash cannot get stuck behind something so that the dog thinks he is being corrected. This is important, especially in the beginning.

With this exercise we make use of the search drive, the pursuit drive, the guarding drive and the survival drive of the dog. The dog will try to devour the prey (the crate), but we want him to bark at it. That is really a bit against his nature. You will have to consistently reward him for the fact that he is not allowed to bite the object, because it is an object which serves as evidence and you cannot allow the dog to destroy the evidence.

There are many roads that lead to Rome, but only one way to teach a dog to retrieve a large object.

It is clear that the dog, while exercising, has to be able to work with all kinds of large objects. All kinds of real live objects have to be included in that list. A handler will have to let his imagination go here and as much as possible copy real life so that the dog is prepared somewhat for that.

3. Retrieving/Searching for a Person

This is really done in the same way as retrieving of a large object and has the same number of sections to be judged, with the understanding that the large object is a "thing" and a person is alive, so there is some difference. Don't start training the dog to retrieve a person until he has learned to retrieve a large object. The dog now gets to do this with a helper, who has to be ready to help the same as he did with the object. First, we introduce the dog to the helper, who has been placed behind a tree, with his back to it, so that the dog learns to look behind things and so he also cannot approach or bite the helper from behind. When the dog has found the helper, command him again *Astor . . . . Loud,* and, in place of the crate, you should now tap the helper.

One of the handiest ways to teach the dog is to use a ball that the helper takes with him. When the dog barks well, the helper will drop the ball and the dog may fetch it. Eventually the dog will understand that he can expect the ball and does not try to bite anymore. When you begin to practice at a greater distance, the helper must take the ball with him. The dog will relate the ball to the helper and will wait until the handler is there. If you are testing the dog's guarding ability and the dog bites, he will then let go on his own, waiting for the ball which then will be given to him promptly. During testing, the helper is dressed in a bitesuit and there is no ball, but the dog will go for that ball anyway because it has become a habit and he does not expect there not to be one. See to it that you have the ball with you and reward him with "great joy" after the exercise.

As training in retrieving people continues, the distance between the handler and his dog continues to increase, although there is still that long leash to encourage the dog and correct him. When the handler comes to the place where the dog finds the man, the leash is picked up to let the dog know that the handler has arrived.

Does the dog make mistakes? If so, return to one of the previous phases and then lead him again in the right direction. Later on, in the more advanced phases of testing, the dog will have to retrieve a person by himself in the woods or guard a person by himself. During the guarding of the find, the helper will start yelling at the dog. The dog then may bite, but it is not necessary. For a sharper dog it is maybe better to teach him not to bite, while for a weaker dog it is maybe good to allow him to bite. There are thousands of variations possible, because there is no dog which is the same, but that also goes for the handlers.

In this case, the dog does not bite a person standing still. Here we make use the long leash and the command not to bite. This command the dog already knows from "bringing articles" and that is why it is so important to teach the dog "bringing articles" forced (under pressure). It is also very important to teach the dog the "transport" exercise after finding the person. The helper has the ball under his left arm and you grasp the man by the right shoulder or you command him to come forward a step or two. You command the dog on the leash to stand the left side of the helper by saying *Astor . . . . Plaats* (i.e., handler – helper – dog) and after that *Astor . . . . Transport* and walk a couple metres with the dog, after which the helper drops the ball for the dog. You stop and let the dog bring you the ball. After this you continue the transport without making use of the ball and stop again a little further with the command, *Astor . . . . Halt*. The exercise is done now and as a reward you throw the ball to the dog once more. It is an excellent way to teach the dog to retrieve and transport. The KNPV Inspection Order has various transport exercises, which we will discuss next. Because of the number of transport exercises and diverse ways to carry them out, the dog's motivation can sometimes weaken or get confused.

4. Transporting a Suspect
The transport exercises are judged as follows:

a. Transport of a suspect
    i. the way the dog did the transport;
    ii. not biting during transport;

     iii. retrieving a small (metal) object that has fallen from the decoy.

b. Transport and re-attack a fleeing decoy
     i. the way the dog did the transport;
     ii. not biting during the transport;
     iii. if he's slow to stop someone;
     iv. releasing;
     v. not biting;
     vi. guarding.

c. Transport designed to test the dog's ability to guard:
     i. the way the dog did the transport;
     ii. not biting during the transport;
     iii. not biting before fleeing;
     iv. making the decoy stop fleeing;
     v. letting go;
     vi. not biting; and
     vii. guarding.

d. Transport with defense of the handler:
     i. the way the dog did the transport;
     ii. not biting during the transport;
     iii. the types of defense;
     iv. letting go;
     v. not biting; and
     vi. guarding.

The transport exercises were meant to be used after the arrest. Long after World War II, a Dutch policeman/doghandler patrolled on a bicycle accompanied by his dog (that's why they have included bicycle work in some of the exercises. Following a bicycle, attacking a suspect on a bicycle and guarding an object are in the inspection programs).

I can remember an incident from 1964, in which I and my first service dog, Astor, stopped a suspect who was drunk and not willing to be brought to the office just a couple of kilometres away. The man, a well-known individual who was always drunk, made such a lot of noise and gestured so much with his arms that the dog thought he had to protect me. When we arrived with the suspect at the police station, the man, who started out with long pants, now had only short pants left. His pants had become prey to the dog. Another case, but not quite as bad as the last one, was that of two Frenchmen in a stolen car. This was with my second service dog, Astor 2, who also did

Transport exercise with "Astor I" on the left side – note that the "suspect" appears to be clutching something in his hand and how focused the dog's attention is. This is a photo of the author as a young handler, sometime in the sixties.

the transport exercise over a few hundred metres to a police car which was ready and waiting for us.

Today the transport is not used any more in real-life situations and it is also the same with other things in the testing program. KNPV became more and more sport. The government took over the whole of the testing program for police work and made a program which is more real to the practice. The KNPV did not change the inspection program and the result was that in fact the KNPV dog is no longer a police dog but a sport dog. Of course, a lot of police officers buy their dog from someone who did KNPV, which is a good basis for a police dog.

Back to a practical part of the KNPV inspection program with an example on guarding an object. I was on the street with my first dog, Astor, and decided to go to a future dog handler's home to drink a cup of coffee. I placed my bicycle against his house, under the window, so that I could see the dog laying down beside the bicycle on the sidewalk. After a while, someone came along the sidewalk in the direction of the bicycle and happened to pass too close. The dog's bite was very serious and the boy had to go to a doctor. Do not say that it won't happen to me, because the unexpected can always come up in the police dog world and, in this case, in the dog's mind, he did what he had to do. It was not his fault, but mine, and so you can learn something with every experience.

Now let's look at a transport with the fallen (or dropped) object. The helper is dressed in the bitesuit and is placed on transport in a given direction and over a certain distance. On signal, the helper drops an object which he had hidden in his left sleeve. The object can be a screwdriver, a closed pocketknife, a key chain, etc. The dog has to watch in such a way that he sees the object drop, picks it up and brings it to the handler, who finishes the transport with the command *Astor . . . . Halt*. The handler takes the object from the dog, who may not bite or chew on it, because it could be important evidence.

When he sees the fallen object, the dog already knows what he has to do, because you already started with the retrieving of a person. The dog then watches the suspect (as he did the helper) because he *expects the ball*. What falls from the suspect is a different object, but that really doesn't matter, because you covered yourself by teaching the dog to apport (pick up and bring the object). Eventually the dog will be fascinated with this also and he will do his work gladly when he notices that he is rewarded for it, and after that he works so that he may play again with the ball. But do not forget to train your dog also to apport all kinds of other objects, such as steel, wood, rubber, etc. The dog really gets to like the ball and you can use that liking in other search work, such as working on drugs, cadavers and explosives.

Of course, the training that was done in the woods or in a building will also apply to open terrain. The transport is an addition to the attack exercise, but it is better to teach the dog the transport exercise separately, as I have outlined. The rest of the information needed to complete the transport exercises will be made clearer during the explanation of position exercises.

The Position Exercises

These exercises can be found on the list of judging, used by the inspectors. They were first listed at the beginning of the section on Division III of the KPNV program in this chapter (E. to M.). They are divided into four sections:

Section A:

5. stopping a man, who defends himself with a stick, the so-called "stick position";

6. refusing the commands of a stranger; and

7. transporting, followed by stopping a fleeing suspect (see transport exercises under 2).

Section B:

8. stopping a man fleeing on a bicycle, the so-called "bicycle position"; and

9. transporting, followed by testing of guarding (see transport exercise under 3).

Section C:

10. stopping a man who shoots a firearm, the so-called "shot position" – the testing of the dog's confidence under fire;

11. stopping a suspect, who is throwing articles at the dog to distract and/or frighten him; and

12. transporting, followed by defending the handler (see transport under 4).

Section D:

13. recalling the dog once he is on his way to attack the suspect.

Earlier I indicated that it is absolutely wrong to teach the dog to bite early in the training program. While the handler, of course, has to know that the dog will do his work under all circumstances, this should have been tested for before the purchase, so that later on you have no surprises. Divisions 1 and 2 of the KNPV program don't require that the dog bite anything (and some require that he be taught *not* to bite certain items). Start with the exercises at a very short distance, so that you can help your dog with the bite work. Let him win the exercises, so that he may become stronger and more confident and let him, by way of that long leash, feel as must as possible that you are there.

Stroke the dog over the head and back, if you use this as a way of encouraging your partner. Use the command *Astor . . . . Vast* when the dog has to bite at a short distance from you on the long leash, and *Astor . . . . Los* if the dog has to stop biting and release the helper. When the dog, at a short distance, understands the basic requirements of the exercise and especially understands *Vast* and *Los*, you can expand the exercise to larger distances.

The most important exercises are 5, 8 and 10, for which the dog has to get 18, 15 and 18 points (see the list). Increase the exercise's frequency, intensity and complexity over a period of time. Much has happened already and it is now that you have to work further in the right direction.

Exercise 5 involves sending the dog to attack a suspect armed with a stick, who will stand still at the last moment and surrender (the helper does not actually attack with the stick in this exercise). Before the handler sends him, the dog will get the normal commands. When the helper stands still, the dog may not bite and has to guard the helper. The exercise is like retrieving in an open field and after the arrest of the helper, the exercise ends with a transport.

Some of the requirements for train-

No tree is too high for "Athos".

ing a dog to attack a suspect on a bicycle (8) are covered in the section on Bitework. It is important to teach the dog to bite the leg, because the helper, if bitten on the arm, can take a serious fall, not to mention fall on top of the dog, and injure either himself or the dog. It is also a good idea to cover the wheels of the bicycle, because a dog that gets caught between the spokes of the bicycle would probably not want to do this exercise again.

As far as exercise 10 goes, the dog has already learned the sound of the gun shot during the exercise "Be Quiet" and should not have any problems here. He should also not have any problems with the difference in the direction the shot comes from between this exercise and and the "Be Quiet" exercise, because the circumstances are totally different. The dog is not so dumb that he will not know how he can get his reward. Do not increase the distance between the handler and the dog too quickly, and especially remember to hold on to the long leash during this training, as the dog will derive some confidence in this reminder of his handler's presence.

All the position exercises start at a designated starting point. After arriving, the handler calls to the helper in the bite suit with the words, *Halt . . . . Police*. This is to be repeated at least twice, after which the dog is sent with the command *Astor . . . . Stellen*. The handler should immediately follow the dog, who has disappeared and locates the helper. The handler is met by the instructor or, when testing, by the inspector, then finishes the exercise while the instructor or the inspector is there by calling the dog back.

Recalling the dog, who is on his way to attack the decoy, needs a little extra attention. The exercise begins in the same manner as the other position exercises, however, now the decoy hides at a distance of approximately 100 metres, after which, from a signal of the instructor/inspector, the dog can be sent to retrieve the decoy/suspect. The handler walks with the dog, no closer nor no further than 10 metres apart, for approximately 60 metres, and the dog has to return quickly and straight to his handler on the command *Astor . . . . Here*.

Again, this is a reminder that this is a sports program and not a practical program. There is no way to send a dog after a suspect in a busy town, with a lot of people on the street, and then try to call him back. This is for use in the field or for sport. However, surveillance can be done, but only on leash. It is good to know how to perform this kind of exercise as a foundation for other training, but it will not happen much in real life that a service dog is used in such a way.

As a hobby, many think it is a great accomplishment and people enjoy it a great deal. Many KNPV dogs are sold to police departments in and outside the country, as I indicated before. If they are then trained further for police work, by people who really know what to do with the dog in certain situations in practice, and there is a certificate awarded by people who really know what "the needs" are, then it is O.K. However, the KNPV program is not really based on real-world usage. Some examples of items missing from the program, which would be of use in police work, include searching in a building and tracking. There is no tracking since 1953 in the program, so that it is not a complete K9 training program anymore.

Beth and "Sammy" doing obstacles, Bellingham, Washington.

General Obedience and the Way to Present the Dog

1. General Obedience

This section is, as I have mentioned earlier, judged over the entire test. That is why it is a very good idea, while you are exercising on the exercise terrain, or wherever you are, to be aware of this section. Mistakes that the dog makes in this respect will not only affect certain exercises, but will also affect the dog's overall score. It is too much to mention where this all happens, since many of the details which affect scoring here will not impact on the dog's working ability, but rather on the general appearance of the exercises. Because of the number of exercises (divisions) in this part of the test, the number of points that can be lost through neglect of this section is 10.

2. The Way to Present the Dog

This section, too, is judged throughout the rest of the tests. All the mistakes the handler makes during the testing program will be marked down in this section. This counts, by the way, whenever the handler fails to do what the inspector explains or says at the beginning of every exercise. These are mistakes you cannot blame on the dog, but are the result of the sloppiness of the handler, and can be seen in the way the dog is presented to a degree. You really have to keep this in mind from the very beginning of the time you start training your dog.

If you keep a close watch on these two sections and you perform according to the instructions, you will find this makes a difference on the inspection list. If you put on your best appearance, if the dog has a good general obedience and if you have taught yourself the way to present your dog, you will be the winner in all aspects of the testing program.

The KNPV Certificates

The certificates you can receive from KNPV are as follows:

1. KNPV Police Dog Certificate 1

This is the basic certificate of the KNPV, and is a pre-requisite of the other certificates. The KNPV Police Dog Certificate

1 is also recognized by the government as valid for Civilian Services, who generally perform guard work in buildings, soccer stadiums, private estates, etc. This certificate is not enough to qualify a dog for police service, as I indicated before.

2. KNPV Police Dog Certificate 2

The certificate, which goes a step higher, by which many try to prove themselves. This is really for people who do not find Police Dog 1 enough. In real life, it is not worth much.

3. Object Guard Dog Certificate

To qualify as a member of the Civilian Protection Services in Government, as well as in the private sector, and to be able to work with a service dog, this certificate is needed. It is the minimum required certificate.

4. Rescue Dog Certificate

This certificate has been added to the KNPV program to train dogs for the location of live people under snow and debris. It is not a Cadaver Dog, which is for finding human beings after they have been dead 2 to 24 hours.

5. Human Scent Discrimination Certificate

This is not recognized by the government, which trains its own dogs for scent discrimination. However, to obtain a KNPV certificate you have to train in:

a. tracking;

b. suspect discrimination;

c. retrieving a person;

d. retrieving a large object;

e. searching on the crime scene; and

f. Division 1 of the KNPV certificate.

Many KNPV members see this as a hobby. It cannot be used in practical police work, because that is not allowed. That has to be done by a police officer with a dog with certificates recognized by the government.

In my book, *My Favorite Judge is Living in a Kennel,* you can read more about these subjects. The training of Cadaver Dogs, Drug-sniffing Dogs and Explosive-detecting Dogs does not exist at KNPV, because as a civilian you cannot get a permit to have in your possession things like drugs or explosives (not to mention the explaining you would have to do if you were found with a corpse in your possession). Also, as a police officer, you have to have a very serious reason to get such a permit. In the Netherlands, and as far as I know also in Germany, having such items in your possession is watched very carefully and it is almost impossible to receive a permit to have such items in your possession. An excellent point of view, if you ask me.

"Aras" of the Joliet Police Department found a few packages of marijuana.

5

In Practice

The Dog as a Means of Warning

The dog, of course, has a tremendous worth as a means of warning. We think of the animal as a guard of our house and yard, as a guide dog for the blind, etc. In the police practice, it is the same. The dog's tremendous senses, such as his nose and his ears, are at his disposal and strongly developed. That, of course, has to do with his survival instincts. When the dog still lived in the wild, another animal might have been too fast for him, had his senses not alerted him to the presence of prey or predator. It is natural for the dog to react very strongly to his senses.

The dog can recognize the footsteps of his master, or of other people who live in the same house. It often happened that my father would come home and our dog knew before us, because he had already heard my father's footstep. I'm certain the dog could recognize the sound of the engine of our car among the sounds of other cars.

A dog is a giant in the way of ability; his capabilities reach much further than we people can imagine, and I have to say that I have been dumbfounded by the possibilities of this olfactory system. The goal of the dog, and his strong urge to survive and reproduce, makes it possible for him to use his olfactory system in the most unlikely ways.

Strong, domineering smells (at least, to a human nose) cannot keep the dog from reaching his goal. The dog is a typical nose animal; the scent organ is the central organ. The hearing and smelling capacities of the dog are without a doubt superior and I can prove it through anecdotes of incidents that occured while I was a policeman.

Once, I was on the night shift, conducting my surveillance on a bicycle. This was in the neighborhood of the ferry over the North Sea canal, the border between my hometown of Zaanstad and our capital, Amsterdam. I was waiting there for the ferry to come ashore when suddenly I noticed that Astor 2, my second service dog, who was laying next to my bicycle, all of a sudden stood up straight and looked in the direction of the embankment which bordered on that canal. Since the largest ammunition dump of the Netherlands was on that wharf, I decided to go and inspect it. Apparently, the dog had heard something, but I did not. I jumped on my bicycle and the dog also seemed to want to go. I had to ride towards the east and around a bend. When I came around the corner, I saw, approximately 100 metres further, by the main entrance to the factory, two security guards from the factory, who had thrown a buoy to two persons who were drowning. They were pulled in by a rope. I helped pull them in and later on, it turned out that they were two drunk sailors, who had fallen in the water there and couldn't swim! Both of them received dry clothing and were brought to the police station where they were able to have a shower. Even though the guards were already there to help, we have to note that the dog was reacting beautifully, even at a distance of 250 metres with the traffic of the ferry and the factory building in between.

This is just a little story about the ears of the dog. The difference of sounds, such as the car of the boss, the bicycle bell or the voice, are identifiable to the dog's ear. That the dog not only hears, but also reacts to the sounds, reinforces my feelings about them. The handler is constantly encouraged to watch the dog during the patrol. That is why patrolling on foot is also encouraged. But more developed than his ears is the nose of the dog. Scents which cannot be detected by people are not a problem at all for the dog. Not much is hidden from him during the patrol with you, because of his excellent developed olfactory system.

With the dog on patrol, whether in the police service or for personal protection, or in the guarding of the house and yard, there is the security for everyone. No one can take that task from the dog and improve on it, of that I am absolutely sure.

The Dog as a Weapon

Keeping in mind that originally the dog was a predator, with this natural instinct to defend himself, the animal is capable of protecting himself and that which belongs to him. Because of that he can also attack, but because he has been domesticated, he also feels subordinate to, and respectful of people. Only the cornered or hungry animal will test the authority of people. The dog has gotten to know people as higher in the chain of command over the centuries. A service dog is definitely one of the least dangerous animals, because the need to bite is kept down because of the urge to be obedient. His aggressiveness has to be in the correct balance with his obedience, and that is why, in the inspection rules, so much attention is given to the obedience and the way of presenting the dog. This makes the dog a great help, if the handler has had good training as well. The handler and the dog have to be a good combination, as we discussed earlier.

However, you should let the dog take the initiative in some circumstances, namely:

a. in defense of the handler;

b. in preventing of the flight of a suspect; and

"Athos de la Tourbiere" in action in Honolulu, Hawaii.

c. in guarding objects.

Allowing the dog to do things on his own initiative is of very great importance, because the dog has the jump on any other weapon. The suspect gets, if everything goes well, the not-asked-for-help of the dog. Most criminals will never forget such an experience and attackers will not try this a second time. The safety of the police officer/dog handler on patrol, as well as the safety of others, especially civilians, is of paramount importance to the dog. The latter will always know that they are supported by the handler and his dog who, in every calamity in the neighborhood, and on the first call, are on the scene of the disaster. The intervention of the patrol dog is not too radical, but it is enough. There are no situations that the dog cannot take care of, while the use of a firearm can be fatal, either to the suspect, innocent bystanders or the police officer. For minor misdemeanors, such as ignoring a barricade or ignoring commands from the police, the dog is an excellent remedy. Once again, the fact is that the use of a dog is less radical. With the dog, the so-called "proportional principle" can always be assured. There will never be more damage than the seriousness of the sentence for the crime.

The Dog as Means of Tracking

Using a similar approach as in the last section, I will explain the use of the dog as a means for tracking, that is, tracking in a police sense. Nowadays criminals are having a field day and the dog can make a tremendous contribution in fighting their activities.

The discovery of the potential of the nose or scenting capabilites of the dog in fighting of criminals was made by Professor Hans Grosz from Grasz, in Austria, in the last years of the previous century. Since that time the dog has allowed himself to be used by people in the fight against criminals.

Early in 1903, the nose of the dog was brought in practice with the scent discrimination of a suspect, who had murdered a servant girl. She was killed with a knife and the dog, Harras, a German Shepherd, brought the knife, because of the scent, back to the suspect, who was punished for the crime. Since that time, dogs have gotten tremendous results when it comes to detecting human scent, and there are many Malinois among the best in the Netherlands. The nose of the Malinois does not have to take a back seat to any dog's. On the contrary, a Malinois is motivated in such a way that, in many cases, he works much better, or at least uses his nose much better, than other breeds. Here in the Netherlands, the Malinois is liked very much as a police dog and the stories about vicious dogs are not true. It is only what you want to hear! Every dog has his own character. They are just like people. Bad dogs are not born, they are made that way by people, who raise and train them.

To be able to smell every footstep and to be able to do it for hours or days gives this dog a great advantage. The nose of the dog is, for people, that beautiful means of help, just like hearing aids, a stethoscope, glasses, a telephone, etc.

In struggling with the criminal element, we are using the nose of the dog as a tool. We are using the nose of the dog to do our smelling for us. Tremendous results are possible in searches for drugs, explosives, cadavers, in rescue work and in other situations.

Conclusion

At the end of my story, I come to the conclusion that the Malinois is very much suited for the work of a police dog, without exception. In some cases, he has an advantage. An example of this is in warm countries, where the Malinois, because he has a lower weight than, for instance, a German Shepherd, can keep going longer.

I showed you his ability as a pedigreed dog and his ability as a mixed breed. The KNPV plays a very important part here, because this association has meant so much in the development of the Malinois in the last 35 years. I have witnessed these developments in the 40 years of my service as a police officer and also as a judge for the Dutch Organization of the Service Dog, the professional opposite of the KNPV, which has added much to those experiences. Many Malinois have passed through my fingers and I really mean it when I say that I do know something about it. I hope I have given the subject some substance and have helped those interested to size themselves up for this kind of work.

While reading this book, you may come to the conclusion that all the police dogs in the Netherlands are Malinois. On the contrary, there are other breeds, like the Dutch Shepherd, the German Shepherd and the Bouvier, although the majority are Malinois.

The good Malinois is a fantastic dog as a pet in your home, but certainly also for use as a police dog.

Index

Retrieve: 34, 37, 42-44, 46,
    56-57, 61, 63, 66, 68-70,
    72, 74-75, 78
Revier: see Search
Reward: 31, 36-39, 42, 45, 50-
    51, 53-54, 58, 62, 65, 67-
    69, 72, 75
Rickets: 18
Rubber ball: 42

S

Scent: 57-59, 78, 84-85
Schofthoogte: 19-20, 22
Search (*Revier, Zoeken,
    Such*): 42-46, 56-59, 63,
    66-68, 72, 76, 78
Shanks: 20
Shoulders: 18-20, 22
Sit (*Zit, Sitz*): 36, 43-44, 50,
    54-57, 60-61
Situational experience: 33-
    35, 47, 53, 61, 72
Size: 15-17, 20, 22
Skin: 18, 20
Skull: 17
Slip chain: 42
Snout: 17, 23
Stay (*Blijf, Bleib, Steh*): 43-
    44, 51, 55-56
Stay Down (without han-
    dler): 50, 52-53, 65
Steel pins (stake): 39, 42, 51,
    61, 65
Steh: see Stay
Stick and the shot test: 27,
    62, 73-75
Stil: 43-44, 54

Stop: 18
Such: see Search
Suitability for police work:
    12, 24, 31
Surveillance: 13, 75, 81
Suspect: 40
Swimming: 46, 60-61

T

Tail: 20, 22, 24
Tattoo number: 26
Teeth: 18, 21-22, 57
Tervuerense shepherd: 10
Thighs: 20, 24
Throat: 18, 24
Tracking: 13, 76, 78, 84
Transport: 46, 63-64, 69-74
Trunk: 19

U

Uitcomen: see Out
Underarms: 18
Upper arms: 18
Upper line: 19

V

Vast . . . apport: see Hold
    Tight
Vast . . . stellen: see Bite
Veterinarian: 26, 28
Voet: see Heel
Voice/tone: 38-41, 53-54, 62,
    69, 82
Volg: see Walk Beside

W

Walk and Talk: 32-36

Printed and bound
in Boucherville, Quebec, Canada by
MARC VEILLEUX IMPRIMEUR INC.
in April, 2000